Devenish Press • Boulder, Colorado

Ireland

Standing Stones to Stormont

Stories and Photographs by Tom Quinn Kumpf

Project Editors: Jan Bachman and Carolyn Eve Green

Design: David Skolkin

Printed in Singapore

10 9 8 7 6 5 4 3 2 1

Library of Congress Catalog Card Number: 2003106487

Devenish Press books are available for special promotions, and to libraries and schools at special rates. For details, contact: 303.926.0378

Limited edition prints of the photographs herein and in all Devenish Press books are available for purchase.

Contact:
DEVENISH PRESS,
P.O. Box 17007,
Boulder, CO 80308-0007, USA
www.devenishpress.com
or
TOM QUINN KUMPF,
P.O. Box 21515,
Boulder, CO 80308-1515, USA
www.tomkumpf.com

page i: Connemara
pages ii–iii: Castle near Ruan

Table of Contents

Foreword

CHILDREN IN IRELAND, North and South, in both public and parochial schools, are taught Irish mythology from the third grade on. However, the stories are not passed on as something strange or peculiar. They are integrated and taught as a very real part of Irish history. Indeed, to say that the stories are fictional accounts designed merely to entertain or inspire would be entirely false. More than one prominent scholar has stated assuredly that great characters such as Cúchulainn, Fionn mac Cumhaill, Conchobar mac Nessa, and Medb, Warrior-queen of Connacht, are a matter of history and really did exist. Many battle sites prove to be true and accurate and it is a matter of written record that the Celtic warriors of the third century found the hills behind the Fergus River at Corofin in County Clare to be garrisoned by Tuatha dé Danann, the people of the goddess Danu, more commonly known as fairy folk.

The volume of literature available as a result of the long course of human habitation on this island is phenomenal and often overwhelming to the person who has never before explored Ireland's past—and I encourage the interested reader to indulge himself as deeply as possible. This work is designed with a focus on Irish identity and how the Irish understand the relationship between themselves and a landscape shaped by an ancient, active past. The reader should also appreciate how significant and close to the surface the Otherworld is in the lives of the people. Recognized as a world running parallel to our own, this spirit realm is separated from us by the thinnest of veils and the Irish, even those who profess total disbelief, still respond to the rhythms of everyday life as if respect for the Good People, or fairy folk, is a fundamental part of living.

This book contains photographs of very real places, some spacious and scenic, others cramped and cluttered, but all fashioned to show how directly the names of places are attached to legend and myth. The accompanying text follows similarly—some sections focus

opposite page:
Legananny Dolmen

Wagon Road

on specific tales and events while some explore matters much more broadly. Others document personal encounters and are the result of observations, interpretation, and emotions I've experienced while working there.

My objective here is to show just how far back the Irish go, and how deeply this sense of identity runs in their hearts. Despite the pride and respect Irish immigrants genuinely feel, their understanding of "Irish," so separated by time and the mixing of other cultures, is murky at best. The identity I speak of here is seasoned, comes through living long on the land, and runs far deeper than most people care to imagine. People who are so accustomed to their own beliefs and attitudes often lose touch with the origins and logic behind many of the things they do daily. I thought I had a real understanding of the Irish following my third and fourth visits, but I was surprised by my lack of knowledge anytime they started to speak to me about things as if I were one of their own. They honor the past, are certainly proud of who they are and what they have become, but many of the Irish don't always recognize how closely tied their past is to their present.

MUCH CAN BE SAID about the richness of literature available, but there are a few points that must be made if the readers are to get the most out of this or other books about Ireland. First, I would ask that the readers do their best to let go of the idea that violence, hot temperedness, and alcoholism are the true marks of an Irishman. The truth is the Irish work hard, long hours; most publicans will not tolerate shouting let alone fighting in the pub; and not only is Ireland's rate of alcoholism the lowest in Europe, it is less than half that of the United States. Unlike most bars in the States, Irish pubs are places where the entire family socializes and, despite what might otherwise be said, that is the real reason every village and town has one. The pubs offer food, drink, and entertainment, and are places where neighbors, including the children, meet for sport, gossip, and banter.

The Irelands of the North and South are different and the people do not see themselves in the same light. To make a very long and complex story short, Northern Ireland and the Republic of Ireland are officially two different countries. The North is made of six counties in the province of Ulster, and is still under the control of Great Britain. The Republic, more popularly known as 'The Free State,' gained its independence in 1922 and consists of the twenty-three counties that make up the provinces of Leinster, Munster, and Connacht, and the three remaining counties of Ulster. Despite what the media says about the ongoing conflict in the North being a religious war between Catholics and Protestants, The Troubles are so much more a war of race and identity between two groups of people who just happen to be Catholic or Protestant. The Catholics are native Irish whose time on the land goes as far back as the beginning, while the Protestants are descendants of English and Scottish immigrants who came to Ireland in the mid-to-late 1600s.

If you were to ask anyone in Catholic West Belfast where they've come from, they'll likely respond with, "This piece of turf, five-thousand years ago, and the dolmen on the hill proves it." For Protestants, however, the answer is a bit more complicated. They may live in Ireland, claim to be Irish when the title seems appropriate, but the connection is hard to satisfy when they associate themselves with Great Britain in so many other ways. Their ancestors came from England and Scotland, so their dolmen is standing on a hill somewhere across the Irish Sea. This is one of the reasons why the recent marches and parades of the Orange Order are so important to them—given the political gains Irish Catholics have made over the past thirty years, Protestants loyal to the Queen are left with little else by way of cultural expression and tradition in Ireland.

By contrast, this situation does not exist in the Republic. The population is almost entirely Catholic and any differences that might exist with a small Protestant population have been worked out over the last eighty-some years. Everyone bears the same political right and the question of identity is not an issue as it is in the North.

Finally, it must be stated that the Romans, for all their worldly conquests, never made it to Ireland. They were stopped at Hadrian's Wall in southern Scotland by the Pics, a warrior tribe who convinced the legions that the tribes in Ireland were extremely violent and uncompromising. The Romans, then, never had a real opportunity to revise and alter what are otherwise wholly Irish or Celtic tales. While it would be an overstatement to suggest that there were no outside influences working on the Irish, even the smallest amount of reading leads one to accept that what is at hand is a collection of literature and stories as rich, pure, and original as anything else available. On the other hand, it would seem equally naïve to think that the peasantry of Ireland, the people who gave these wonderful stories of Cúchulainn, Fionn, and so many others to Yeats and Lady Gregory, actually provided them with all the elements and principles the tales originally held. Though Yeats and the good Lady may

have been genuinely selfless and well-meaning, they were members of the gentry, the landed aristocracy, and held the lives of the peasantry in their hands. Thus, I think it fitting to presume that they were neither trusted nor very well liked and were given only those features of a story that the storytellers felt were appropriate and harmless to reveal. The tales were not given lightly and this, of course, leaves us to wonder how much substance and beauty was lost to the fear and apprehension of the time.

THE IRISH HAVE ALWAYS UNDERSTOOD and accepted that they are different from other groups of people, but the measure of difference did not reveal itself until Irish Americans began arriving in droves looking for their "Irish roots." Most Irish Americans believe that the Irish are much like them, but there is little truth in this. The native Irish live in two Irelands—the earthly and the divine—and nearly every feature of their existence is shaped by these worlds.

Understanding needs no explanation and often what is known and understood, instinctively or otherwise, quite simply cannot be explained. To explain something is to be subjective

Ardgroom Stone Circle

and limiting, all too often ending up in rationalization that engages the ego and buries the truth in spite of the best intentions. To understand is to know, and that is the last necessary step toward acceptance. To accept something, then, however irrational, is to open that realm and all of its possibilities to further exploration. I have seen and experienced things that logic says could not have happened — impossible sights and manifestations that cannot be explained. Nevertheless, there is no doubt in my mind that they indeed happened. I witnessed them sure and sober and so, despite an educated, rational, analytical mind, I recognize and appreciate that they are real. I sometimes find myself awake in bed in the middle of the night, wondering if the events of my life are really as I remember them. I find it entirely healthy to question, but I also know. Instinct and the senses often supplant logic. Nothing more is needed. Nothing more is obliged.

Tom Quinn Kumpf
April 15, 2003

Doo Lough

Vacation Cottages, Ring Fort

The Mórrígan

Introduction

According to the talk of people who think in Irish . . . . — W. B. Yeats

Cesair, the Partholonians, the Nemedians, the Fomorians, and the Fir Bolg . . . . were the first to inhabit the island, but it was the Tuatha dé Danann, the children of the goddess Danu, known also as the Lords of Light, who would be lifted forever to the mystic realm of gods and goddesses. Disguised as a supernatural race of wizards and magicians, they came from the air to inhabit Ireland well before written history and the arrival of the Celts. With them they brought four treasures: a stone of virtue and destiny called the Lia Fáil, a sword that was inescapable once drawn, a spear of victory, and an ever-filling cauldron that left anyone who ate from it completely satisfied.

Legend tells us they lived within the great mound at Brug na Bóinne, and the Dagda, the Good God, was their father and chief. It was a time when gods and men walked the earth together. They were not limited or separated by the distances between the heavens and the earth. They lived and fought together side-by-side. They developed sacred bonds and over time interbred and shared offspring. When gods and men came together they did so as equals. As Lady Gregory recorded in *Of Gods & Fighting Men* and, as in many circles of Ireland it is still believed, "There is not a king's son or a prince or a leader of the Men of Ireland, without having a wife or a mother or a foster-mother or a sweetheart of the Tuatha dé Danann."

The *Táin Bó Cuailnge* speaks of an Ireland full of magic and imagination and is the oldest native epic in Western literature. The book describes the exploits of Cúchulainn, the warrior hero of Irish myth and legend. Conceived in a union between a mortal woman and a warrior king of the Tuatha dé Danann, his exciting though short life was spent moving in and out of relationships with mortals and gods. He was strong, noble, and extremely handsome, and all the women of Ireland, girls and goddesses alike, were constantly seeking his favor. One of the accounts in the book describes his wonder over the mystical beauty of the land while he was on a quest that was part of his initiation as a warrior. The journey carried him from one end of the island to the other and Ibar, his trusty charioteer, pointed out all the important structures and high places of Ireland. They looked to the Hill of Tara and its magical Stone of Destiny, the great druid mounds of Knowth and Dowth, the many circles and standing stones, and the magnificence of Brug na Bóinne, the place of his conception and the astronomical marvel known to us today as Newgrange.

Today there are remnants of more than 50,000 stone circles in Ireland alone. There also are 30,000 ráths and ring forts, and an incredible number of dolmen, wedge tombs, and lone standing stones. Many are carved with spirals and other ancient designs and appear to be aligned to the sun, moon, or other specific astrological events. Though far short of these numbers, similar structures dot the landscapes of England, Scotland, Wales, and Brittany and are found across North Africa, Siberia, India, China, and in several locations in the Americas. These structures are the very same that drove Cúchulainn on his quest for greatness. They go back a long way, many given form and life thousands of years before Cúchulainn and the Celts appeared on the scene. Indeed, Newgrange was built as a celestial observatory around 3500 B.C. and predates the Pyramids by nearly 1,000 years.

Stone circles, with magical names like Ardgroom, Drombeg, Knocknakilla, Beltany, Carrigagulla, Carrowmore, Killycluggin, Derreenataggart, Drumskinny, and Ballynoe are places of power and pure spirit. No one knows for certain who built these fascinating structures. They

Drombeg Stone Circle

Giant's Ring

are known to us only as the Megalithic People, tribes who inhabited the region thousands of years before Christ. It was a time when shaman, wizards, and chieftains were understood to be half-god half-mortal and what they left behind speaks of a people well aware of their environment, both earthly and celestial.

The Celts, like these ancients before them, held ceremonies at the sites. Some were places of offering and prayer, others sites for celebrations and fairs. Still others were places where people practiced bloodletting and druid magic. It is known that many of the sites are designed around the seasons, most commonly aligned to the solstices and equinoxes. Stone circles in general, but ring forts in particular, are still regarded by many local inhabitants as vents to the Otherworld, places where fairies dwell, and are treated with much caution and respect.

As surely as the gods created man, man has been recreating his gods ever since, and the mists of time thicken or thin according to how men perceive their gods. As life becomes more orderly, more serious, more deliberate, the old order sinks further and further away. With the arrival of the Celts, the gods of old were replaced by other gods—familiar, still earthly, but of a different order. It was a time when the reach of men's souls was constantly shifting between the magic in myth and legend and what they understood to be harsh and real in their world. And, with the coming of Patrick, the gods of help and harassment gave way to yet another: one more stern, demanding, and vengeful. A shadow of Christ arrived, but not before the Dagda and his Tuatha dé Danann went underground to become the *sídhe*,

Turoe Stone

or fairy folk, while men continued to make what they could of life in an ever-changing world.

Ireland, North and South, is a land of strength, of resonance, of life. Every square inch of Irish turf has been pressed flat by the tread of a human foot. Every mountain and lough has been host to a hero. Every new scene draws the soul to another. And, in Ireland especially, every place-name is linked to some special character or event in the past. Poetry and myth are wedded to the land and the people. Every smile reveals a secret. Every tear is worth a tale. Every square inch has experienced human life and death, but the living, the extent of the living, is what shows through.

The moments that are will someday be the times that were. Ireland was formed in the unsettled mists of windy places and humid light, in a dream-time, and today, the native Irish, capable and educated as they are, continue to tell their tales with all the character and conviction of Rhodes scholars. The Dagda, Cúchulainn, and all the other personages of the past still inhabit the soul of this land. The Irish, even through their daily activities, continue to seek what remains of the sacred in the midst of all that has been made otherwise mundane.

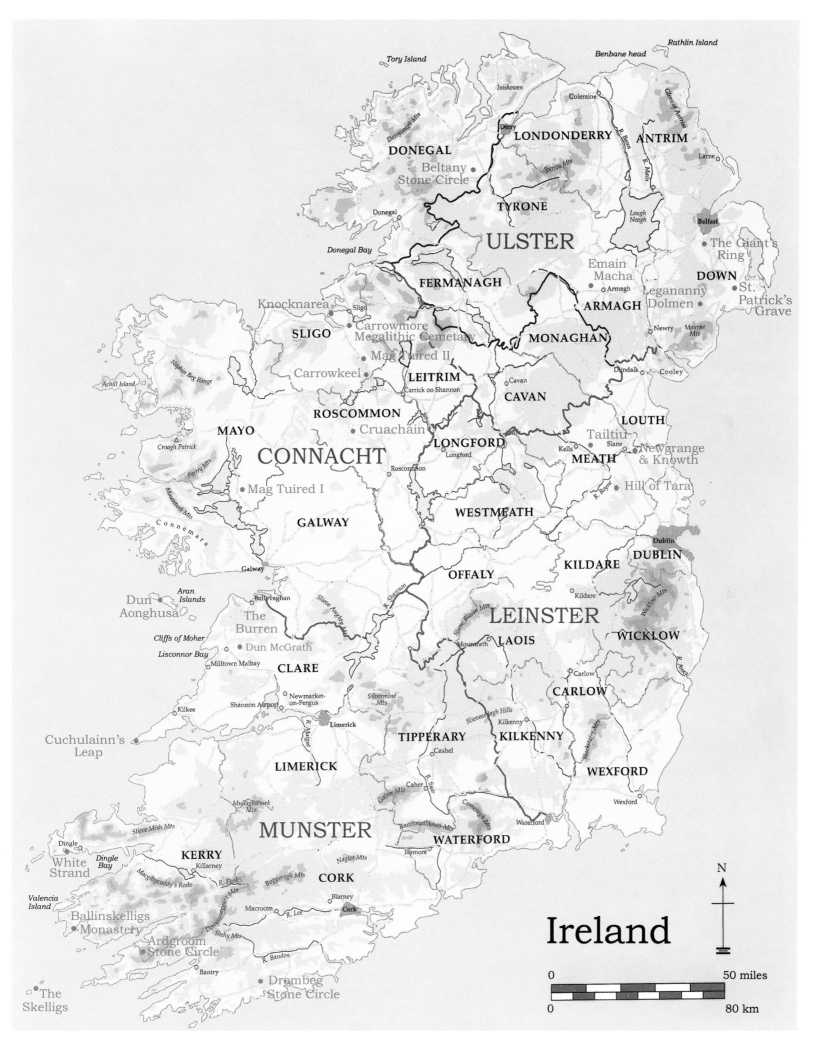

Ireland

Tory Island

Benbane head

Rathlin Island

Inishowen

Coleraine

Derryveagh Mts

Derry

LONDONDERRY

Clens of Antrim

ANTRIM

R. Bann

DONEGAL

Beltany
Stone Circle

Sperrin Mts

R. Main

Larne

TYRONE

Lough
Neagh

Belfast

Donegal

ULSTER

The Giant's
Ring

Donegal Bay

FERMANAGH

Emain
Macha

DOWN

Armagh

Leganamny
Dolmen

St.
Patrick's
Grave

Knocknarea

Sligo

ARMAGH

Carrowmore
Megalithic Cemetary

MONAGHAN

Newry

Mourne
Mts

SLIGO

Mag Tuired II

Dundalk

Cooley

Nephin Beg Range

Carrowkeel

LEITRIM

Cavan

Achill Island

ROSCOMMON

Carrick on Shannon

CAVAN

LOUTH

Cruachain

Tailtiu

MAYO

LONGFORD

Slane

Newgrange
& Knowth

Croagh Patrick

CONNACHT

Roscommon

Longford

Kells

MEATH

R. Boyne

Partry Mts

Mag Tuired I

Hill of Tara

Mweelrea Mts

WESTMEATH

Connemara

GALWAY

Dublin

DUBLIN

KILDARE

Galway

OFFALY

Kildare

Wicklow Mts

Aran
Islands

Ballyvaghan

Slieve Aughty Mts

R. Shannon

LEINSTER

Dun
Aonghusa

Slieve Bloom Mts

WICKLOW

Cliffs of Moher

The
Burren

LAOIS

Lisconnor Bay

Dun McGrath

Mountrath

Carlow

R. Slaney

Milltown Malbay

CLARE

Blackstairs Mts

Kilkee

Newmarket-
on-Fergus

Silvermine
Mts

Carlow

CARLOW

Shannon Airport

Slievearlagh Hills

Kilkenny

Cuchulainn's
Leap

R. Maigue

Limerick

TIPPERARY

Kilkenny

KILKENNY

WEXFORD

LIMERICK

Cashel

R. Suir

Mullaghareirk Mts

Galtee Mts

Caher

Wexford

Slieve Mish Mts

MUNSTER

Knockmealdown Mts

Comeragh Mts

Waterford

Dingle

Nagles Mts

WATERFORD

KERRY

Killarney

CORK

Lismore

White
Strand

Dingle
Bay

Macgillycuddy's Reeks

R. Flesk

Boggeragh Mts

Blarney

Valencia
Island

Derrynasaggart Mts

Cork

Ballinskelligs
Monastery

Macroom

R. Lee

Ardgroom
Stone Circle

Shehy Mts

R. Bandon

Bantry

Drombeg
Stone Circle

The
Skelligs

N

0   50 miles

0   80 km

XXIII

Books, Battlefields, and Tír na nÓg

THE *LEBOR GABÁLA ÉRENN*, or The Book of the Taking of Ireland, is a collection of stories from various periods of early Irish history. Known also as The Book of Invasions or The Book of Conquests, the stories attempt to combine myth, legend, and the earliest Irish genealogies within the margins of medieval biblical thought. Written in the twelfth century, the manuscript begins with the arrival of Cesair, a granddaughter of Noah, who went to Ireland to escape the great flood when she was denied entrance to the ark. The book lists the characteristics of each of the invading tribes, the order in which they arrived in Ireland, and ends with the coming of the Milesians, more commonly known today as the Celts.

A significant portion of the book focuses on the Tuatha dé Danann and the magical period of time they ruled Ireland. Understood to be a supernatural race of wizards and magicians, their divine origins are clearly implied in the text. They arrived as smoke from the air on a mountain in the West just before Beltaine (May 1), and show themselves superior to all other peoples of the earth in their mastery of all arts. They defeated a short, dark race of men called the Fir Bolg in the first battle of Mag Tuired and then went on to take control of Ireland with the defeat of the Fomorians, a magical though violent race of pirates often associated with sea deities, at the second battle of Mag Tuired.

Afterward, the Fir Bolg fled to the more distant parts of Ireland, some settling on Rathlin Island and in the more remote sections of Connacht, but the Aran Islands ultimately became their home. Dún Aonghusa, a large stone cliff fort located on Inishmore and one of Ireland's main tourist attractions, was named for their leader, Angus.

The Fomorians suffered great slaughter and were driven back into the sea. The Tuatha dé Danann went on to establish Tara as their seat of power and are credited with building many

"So I says to your man, 'You may hold the paper to that land well enough, but 'tis an ill wind you'll be riding forever if you go digging around that old ring fort.'"

—Overheard in a pub, Ennistymon, Co Clare, 2001

opposite:
Ulster Way, Co. Down

Mag Tuired I Battle Cairn

Mag Tuired II

of Ireland's ancient ruins. Under their rule, Ireland experienced 297 years of peace and prosperity until, ultimately, the Milesians defeated them on the plain at Tailtui and changed the face of Ireland forever.

THE FIRST BATTLE OF MAG TUIRED is marked today by an immense stone cairn just outside the village of Cong in County Mayo. After 105 days of posturing and preparation, the Fir Bolg and Tuatha dé Danann came together in a clash that was heard all over Ireland. The battle raged for four days and in the end the Fir Bolg suffered terrible defeat. It was at this site that the Fir Bolg lost their king, Eochaid, and where their greatest warrior, Sreng, cut off the hand of Tuatha dé Danann King Nuadu. The sword stroke deposed him of his kingship, Nuadu having to follow a dé Danann law that said no king could rule who had suffered a wound or blemish. Later on, a silver hand was fashioned for him by Credne, the chief artificer of the Tuatha dé Danann.

The greatest warrior champion of the Tuatha dé Danann, Bres, assumed the throne and ruled Ireland for seven years. His mother was dé Danann but his father was a chief of the Fomorians. Bres angered the people by favoring his father's kin, but also because they found him inhospitable and mean-spirited. Bres honored neither friend nor stranger and this, considered a disgrace by the people, caused them to cry out for his removal. However, his most unforgivable act, insulting a poet, proved to be his undoing. The people drove Bres from the throne and out of Ireland and Nuadu, subsequently known as Aírgetlám ('of the Silver Hand') assumed the throne once again.

After a time, Bres gathered an invasion force of Fomorians and headed back to Ireland. Their numbers were said to be so great that the sea was filled with ships from Ireland to the Hebrides. They landed and met the Tuatha dé Danann for the second battle of Mag Tuired, located on a plain above Lough Arrow in County Sligo. The Tuatha dé Danann triumphed once again, killing the Fomorians in great numbers, and drove them out of Ireland forever. Today the plain is marked by several cairns, pillar-stones, and a few historical markers that are all but lost to hedge and grasses growing along fence lines. Nevertheless, legends live on, and it is understood that this ground is where the famous Fomorian chief, Balor of the Evil Eye, died by a stone (or a special ball made from a mixture of limestone and the mashed brains of an enemy) cast by the sling of Lug, one of the greatest heroes of the Tuatha dé Danann and Balor's very own grandson. Unfortunately, Balor took the life of King Nuadu before being killed himself.

TAILTIU IS MARKED by a large circular mound near the modern village of Teltown, situated between Navan and Kells in County Meath. Finding the exact location of the battleground was something of a challenge, given all the lanes and hedgerows running across the countryside, and then, in true Irish fashion, the site proved inaccessible due to a large herd of cattle. Made up mainly of immature bulls, they appeared less than accepting of human presence.

Tailtiu, named for a Queen of the Fir Bolg, is famous for being the location of one of the three great fairs of ancient Ireland. Queen Tailtiu led her people in clearing the forest and creating what is still considered some of the best agricultural land in Ireland. The process eventually became so burdensome that it broke her heart and on her deathbed she asked that a fair of feasting and games be held on the grounds each year at the time of Lughnasa (August 1), one of four major celebrations marking the ancient Irish calendar. People came from all over Ireland and, in time, Tailtiu grew to match Tara in size and prominence.

Cows at Tailtiu

Cruachain, Medb's Fort

Nevertheless, the plain proved to be a great place to fight as well. The mortal Milesians and the Tuatha dé Danann came together in battle with massive losses on both sides. The Milesians were victorious, but rather than carry on the slaughter, they offered the surviving dé Danann a way out. A deal was struck where the two sides agreed to divide Ireland in equal halves, but the dé Danann realized too late that they had been tricked. Instead of a division North and South or East and West, the Milesians and their progeny would thereafter live in sunshine and light on the surface of the world, while the Tuatha dé Danann, as immortals, would occupy the dark, sunless places below the surface of land and sea to become the *dés sídhe*, or people of the fairy mound. Despite being tricked, the Tuatha dé Danann remained honorable and true to their word, thereafter responding to humans in kind. They lived strong in the minds of men, but, so it is told, as time went by and generations passed, people thought less and less about them and the less people thought, the smaller and less powerful they became, shrinking from the size and stature of giants to mere wisps of smoke.

THERE ARE MANY THEORIES as to the origin of the fairies, but their connection to the Tuatha dé Danann is the one most accepted and understood by antiquarians and common folk alike. The *Book of Armagh*, written around A.D. 807, says they are the ancient gods of the earth. Some people consider them the gods of pagan Ireland, potent and powerful until they were cast into the dark places by St. Patrick. For others, especially the oldest of old-timers, they are fallen angels whose sin against God was serious enough to keep them out of heaven, but not so grave as to land them all in hell.

The Irish word for fairy is *sídheóg*, or more commonly, *sídhe* (shee). Fairies are *daoine sídhe*, the fairy folk, or *áes sídhe*, people of the fairy mound, or more commonly, *daoine maithe*, the Good People. They can assume just about any shape or size that suits them and possess a special power called *féth fiada*, a mist or veil that renders them invisible or allows them to assume animal form. They spend their time fighting, feasting, and making love and their enthusiasm for music and dance far exceeds that of mortal men. The leprechaun is the only one among them who works, a shoemaker kept busy by fairies who constantly wear out their shoes dancing.

Janus Stones

Fairy Hill

May Eve and November Eve, the nights before Beltaine and Samain, are great festival times for the fairies. On these two nights, they are said to troop and parade across the surface of the land and, from dusk to dawn, both worlds belong to them. Even today, and especially in the countryside, people will not set foot outside after dark on these two nights unless they absolutely must.

Retribution aimed at humans can come in the form of a fairy blast, a sudden gust of wind that destroys property and renders people helpless; a fairy mist that causes people to wander astray; fairy darts that cause pain and swelling in joints, hands, or feet; or a fairy stroke, an abrupt seizure that affects both humans and animals and is, in fact, the origin of the term 'stroke' so commonly used to explain the paralysis and speech difficulties that result from a cerebral hemorrhage. Fairies are also known to snatch humans away—sometimes women, but more often newborns and young children. Their blood is said to be green, a thick gel much like the substance in which frogs lay their eggs. It is also well understood that only people with red blood can get into heaven. Consequently, fairies are constantly stealing, tending, and mating with humans in the hope that their blood will change just enough to allow them a place in heaven on Judgment Day.

Clonmacnois

Fairies will ruin crops, cause milk cows to go dry, burn the occasional house, and strike back in a thousand other ways. More seriously, people die when tractors roll, outbuildings collapse, and cars run into trees. Clearly, the Irish do not believe that all accidents are caused by fairies, but questions to that effect always seem to be lurking somewhere in the background, especially when the circumstances surrounding the death seem the slightest bit strange. People will dig into every aspect of the victim's recent past and, if the incident is alleged to be retribution by the fairies, the people will hold the victim responsible. They will never fault, let alone condemn, the fairies.

Their half of Ireland is known as Tír na nÓg, the Land of the Ever-Young, which many legends place off the West Coast at Liscannor Bay, just south of the Cliffs of Moher in County Clare. On the other hand, most anyone will tell you that their gateways, the vents to the Otherworld, are located in ring forts and other ancient structures. Fairies are thought to live in trees as well, specifically oak and ash, while the lone whitethorn in the center of a field marks fairy paths and places where they rest, feast, dance, and make love. This tree is

Cliffs of Moher from the Sea

considered most dangerous and is not to be tampered with. Hazel is thought to be so revered by the fairies that it is not often burned. The tree was considered sacred to poets, while the fruit of the plant, often described as 'nuts of wisdom,' are deemed to hold magical properties that inspire one to insight and extrasensory perception. The wood of ash and birch are said to ward off fairies. The Good People do not much like to be talked about and milk is the most common way to soothe any nerves that might have been irritated during a session of storytelling.

The native Irish recognize and respect this Otherworld and even the worst skeptics, once they've relaxed enough or trust that the listener will not think them foolish, will offer a word of warning or have a tale or two to tell. To most Americans, fairies are cute little pixies that flit and flirt around and grant the fortunate man his wishes. They are little more than characters in children's tales and the visitor to Ireland can drive the locals mad in moments with all their babbling about The Little People, lucky charms, and rainbows. The likes, dislikes, and concerns of the fairies are understood to be not all that different from our own. Our worlds may occasionally clash, but they are never in conflict. As with everything else Irish, respect is fundamental. The fairies are another tribe—of wizards or earth spirits or ancient gods—but they are an integral part of a history, a force to be reckoned with, even in the modern Ireland of higher education and technology.

Queen's Gardens, Belfast

Cathair Mhic Neachtain Law School

Names, Places, and the Lords of Light

IRELAND IS DIVIDED INTO FOUR PROVINCES and thirty-two counties. These then are broken into baronies and parishes, which are further reduced to include some 60,000 townlands. These sections represent the smallest official units in the country, but each and every townland is divided, officially or not, into even smaller pieces, running somewhere between 30 and 800 more particulars per townland. This amounts to an incredible number of pieces, certainly many million, and each and every one is known by a distinct, specific name.

Much has been written about the relevance and nature of place-names in Ireland. The majority of them are simple terms that describe the physical features of the landscape—mountains, rivers, valleys, etc.—but others come to us after heroes and villains, gods and goddesses, battles and other events, and any number of combinations that made sense or struck the fancy of the people who named them. While place-names are common throughout the world, few people can top the Irish when it comes to the use of wit and imagination in their representation of the land and its lore.

The two most common words in the naming of towns and villages are Bally, and Kil. Bally is the anglicized spelling for *Baile*, which means 'homestead' or 'small settlement.' Likewise, Kil is Cill, meaning 'church.' Thus, any name that opens with Bally speaks of a place that began as a homestead. Any name that begins with Kil or Kill tells us that there is, or once was, a church at that location. Ballyquin, then, translates quite simply as 'Quin's homestead,' while Ballyvangour or, in Irish, Baile Bheanna Gabhar, describes the 'homestead of the peaks of the goats.' Kilmore is simply 'big church,' while Kilfenora, or Cill Fhionnúrach, describes the 'church of the fertile land on the brow of the hill.'

Dun means 'fort' and Drum is a 'ridge.' Thus, the town of Dundrum translates 'fort of the ridge.' Dungall means 'fort of the strangers,' Dun Laoghaire is 'Laoghaire's fort,' while

"The mountain there, and the tomb, are things that truly deserve respect. It's been there a long, long time and, whether you believe in Queen Medb or not, you gotta respect that somebody thought enough to carry all those many stones to the top."

—*A professor from Trinity University in the carpark below Knocknarea, 1999.*

opposite:
Connor Pass

Caherconlish speaks of the 'stone fort of the head of the ford.' Here, another feature of Irish place-names must be mentioned. As the word Caher relates to 'stone forts' in particular, one could mistakenly assume that Dun is an all-purpose term used to identify forts in general. Nothing is ever quite that plain or simple with the Irish and their place-names are often designed to convey information regarding status, class distinction, and any number of other things. Although the majority of forts in Ireland are made of stone, the word Dun is more commonly used because it is a prestige term usually applied to the dwellings of kings and chieftains. Such subtleties weave in and out of the language, particularly in place-names that predate written history. Unfortunately, the original meaning of so many place-names has either been severely distorted or lost forever. The passage of time, a censorious Christian church, and the forced Anglicization of the language during 800 years of British occupation have each taken their toll. The damage is significant, and it takes someone with a vast knowledge of the language and local history to provide a reasonably comprehensive translation of even the most simple word combinations.

BRUG NA BÓINNE means 'hostel of the Boyne' and is the ancient Irish name for Newgrange. This great passage mound, most famous of all Megalithic sites in Ireland, is said to have been the legendary home of Elcmar, King of the Tuatha dé Danann, his wife Boand, the divine personification of the River Boyne, and the Dagda, most prominent of the older Irish gods.

Newgrange Passage Mound

Newgrange Entrance

Considered a palace of the Otherworld, it was a place of endless delight and revelry. Within the mound grew three sacred trees that were never without fruit. Also housed there was one of the four great treasures of the Tuatha dé Danann: an inexhaustible cauldron that left anyone who ate from it completely satisfied.

Newgrange, along with two similar structures called Knowth and Dowth, make up the Boyne River Valley complex and are solar constructs designed sometime between 3700 and 3200 B.C. to align with specific celestial events. Newgrange is aligned to the position of the rising sun on winter solstice. The interior of the chamber is lined with elaborately engraved stones, whose mystery and magic come to life when a shaft of sunlight snakes down the passage to illuminate the rear of the chamber for a scant 17 minutes of the 525,960 minutes that make up a year.

Newgrange Carving

Newgrange Kerbstones

The main passage at Dowth is aligned to receive the light that same day at sunset, marking the longest night of the year, thus explaining the ancient Irish name, Dubad, or 'darkness.' A second passage was designed to catch the cross-quarter sunsets of November 8 and February 4, the ancient festivals of Samain and Imbolc. Unfortunately, this passage was sealed during a recent reconstruction project and is no longer in use.

Knowth is the largest passage mound in Ireland and, like Dowth, is equipped with two separate passages. Positioned directly opposite each other, they mark the spring and autumn equinox, one at sunrise, the other sunset. The interior of Knowth holds the largest collection of Megalithic art in Europe. In the central chamber of the eastern passage is a stone on which is carved a symbol curiously unlike the spirals, crescents, and the other geometric

Knowth

figures around it. In 1999, a researcher placed a drawing of the symbol over a photograph of the full moon and saw that they lined up perfectly. Although this is still a subject of much debate, the stone may well represent the oldest map of the moon known to man, predating Leonardo de Vinci's 1505 drawing by nearly 5,000 years. Even more fascinating is how the symbol is positioned at the very back of the chamber. On those nights when the moon and passage are aligned, the moon's light would have entered the chamber to shine upon an exact image of itself.

In ancient Irish the mound is called Cnogba, so named for its association with Englic, daughter of Elcmar and lover of Angus Óg, son of Dagda, the Good God of the Tuatha dé Danann and Brug na Bóinne, a rather elaborate though marvelous way of indicating its connection to Newgrange.

All other begetting aside, Knowth, Dowth, and Newgrange are each surrounded at their base by large kerbstones, many of them decorated with symbols much like those found inside the mounds. Outwards, and often a fair distance away, are individual 'outliers,' standing stones so positioned that their shadows fall upon particular lines and symbols carved in the kerbstones at specific dates of the year. The main structure of Knowth is bordered by no fewer than seventeen smaller satellite mounds, several having passages and alignments of their own. Similar constructs exist throughout Ireland, but following extensive restorations, the passage mound at Newgrange is clearly the most celebrated and well-known.

THE PASSAGE TOMBS OF CARROWKEEL, or the 'narrow quarter,' are located in the Bricklieve Mountains in County Sligo. Often described as 'chambered cairns,' the remains of fourteen

Carrowkeel Passage Tombs

such structures lie along a narrow ridge overlooking Lough Arrow and the broad expanse of hills and valleys to the northwest. These cairns are not nearly as large as the mounds in the Boyne River Complex and squeezing through the narrow entrances and short passages on hands and knees can pose a real problem for anyone with the willies for tight spaces. On the other hand, they are well off the normal tourist path, seldom suffer more than a few visitors a day, and with no one there to manage or restrict one's movements, one is free to explore the site at leisure. They are thought to be older than the Boyne River Complex by 700 years and are considered to be the oldest man-made rooms on the planet.

Groups of Megalithic monuments are generally identified by letters instead of numbers. The cairns at Carrowkeel are designed to work in combination and together they satisfy a

number of select alignments. Cairns G and K are set to allow sunlight to enter the chamber for several weeks on either side of the summer solstice. Cairn G, however, was built to include a 'light box,' a narrow slit set over the entrance that also directs the light of the setting full moon into the chamber on either side of the winter solstice. Light boxes are both sophisticated and rare, Newgrange being the only other known site in the whole of Ireland to have one. The box transforms the light that passes through it into a focused beam and directs it to specific stones in the chamber of the cairn. Calculating solar alignments may seem hard enough, requiring years of careful observations to be certain the specific days to be marked in the year-long cycle are accurate. Lunar alignments, however, are significantly more complicated. A monthly cycle may only take twenty-eight days to complete, but the date of the full moon, though predictable, shifts continually from month to month. Because of this, the observation time that must have been required to satisfy the lunar alignments at Carrowkeel seems all the more remarkable. Cairn G is designed so that the light box faces the most northerly point the setting moon reaches on the western horizon, an event that only happens once every eighteen and six-tenths years.

Cairn G was built with one other incredible feature. A small vertical slit was carved in the top-center portion of the door slab that stands directly in front of the entrance. The light directed by the light box would settle on a special stone at the very rear of the chamber, a stone covered with small mica crystals and so positioned to reflect the light back through the slit in the door. Some local people believe that these ancient architects wanted to send a bit of the light back to the heavens from which it came. More than likely, however, the slit served as a kind of beacon for the groups of people observing the event from outside the cairn, they too wanting a bit of magic for themselves.

THE STONE CIRCLE OF BALLYNOE, meaning 'new homestead,' is one of the truly great rings of Ireland. Located in County Down, the size and design suggests that upwards of 150 people would have fit comfortably inside the circle during ceremonies and astrological observations. Built sometime around 3000 B.C., the portal stones are set to align with a peak in the Mourne Mountains, some fifteen miles distant, when the midwinter sun sets.

Ballynoe Stone Circle

Carrowmore Megalithic Cemetery

In the very center of the circle are the remains of an oval-shaped cairn. Excavations in 1937 and 1938 unearthed the cremated bones of several young adults. Also found were three egg-shaped stones called baetyls, literally 'sacred meteoric stones,' buried under the surface just outside the cairn. One can only imagine what went through the minds of the men who shaped the stones, but it is clear that they recognized their special nature and heavenly origin.

CARROWMORE, or 'big quarter,' is the earliest known inhabited site in Ireland. Evidence indicates that communities existed here in the Middle Stone Ages, nearly 9,000 years ago. One of County Sligo's many treasures, Carrowmore is home to the largest Megalithic cemetery in Europe, with sixty sites surviving an original number of a hundred or more. Concentrated in an area a bit over one-and-a-half miles long by three quarters of a mile wide, the cemetery contains dolmen, wedge tombs, chambered cairns, standing stones, and stone circles. Several of the monuments are believed to be aligned to specific solar and lunar events.

A FEW MILES DISTANT, but visible from Carrowmore, a huge cairn stands on the very top of a flat, steep-sided mountain called Knocknarea. Translated from the Irish, Mescán

Meadhbha, or 'Medb's Lump,' this giant chambered cairn is said to be the tomb of Queen Medb. Although it has never been excavated, it is believed that a chambered tomb on the scale of Newgrange lies buried beneath. The locals will tell you that no one is willing to risk the wrath of Medb by disturbing her resting place and, so far, that reasoning has worked well enough. There is a large boulder just outside the circle of the cairn that may very well mark the location of a passage entrance. The boulder is situated on the western side of the cairn and is carved with several suncups and lines that appear to form the head of a spear. The cairn is covered with 40,000 tons of white quartz carried in baskets to the top of this mountain some 8,000 years ago from a quarry nearly 100 miles away. Little compares to a walk up the mountain on a warm spring day, especially given the views of Bammisodare Bay and the middens at Cullenamore on Sligo's northwest coast. Local custom claims that people are double-blessed who so honor Medb by dropping a stone from the base of the mountain on the very top of her tomb. I placed a pebble in my pocket and headed for the top.

The climb took longer than expected and, although the sky was clear and bright, the day was growing late and I was forced to photograph the mound as best I could while watching the sun dip ever closer to the horizon. The light readings my camera relayed didn't seem

Knocknarea, Medb's Tomb

right; the meter said there was more ambient light than my many years of shooting would allow me to believe. I shot with all three camera bodies and the meters were all over the place. Consequently, I compensated by taking many more images than normal, under- and overexposing each frame in turn.

I climbed to the top of the cairn and deposited my stone. But, on the way down, a golf ball sized chunk of quartz loosened by my step rolled onto the grass at the base of the mound. I considered and argued and, even though I know it wasn't necessarily the proper thing to do, I was so taken with this site and all it represents, I just couldn't resist. I placed the stone in my bag and removed a coin I had carried in my pocket for nearly thirty years. I took a deep breath and slid the coin into a small gap between two small boulders on the cairn, hoping that the giving of the one would balance the taking of the other.

The surface of the stone was dark and dull when I got it home, but a good cleaning revealed a mass of tiny crystals beneath the dirt and lichen I'd removed. Months later, while writing at the table where the stone then lived, I moved a stack of books and the sun struck the crystals in a dazzling display that lit up the entire room. My mind flashed back to Knocknarea and the great cairn of Medb. I thought of the camera readings my instincts had opposed and how the angle of the setting sun reflecting off of that immense pile of crystal, now dulled by time, may have had everything to do with them. I then imagined how the cairn must have looked when the 40,000 tons of quartz was fresh and new. An image of a huge beacon flashed through my mind, the cairn pulsing and glowing as the light followed the angle of dusk and dawn. The stone had told its story, making it perfectly clear why the ancients were so often referred to as the Lords of Light.

Circles, Stones, and Healing Wells

Many of the explanations regarding the origin of stone monuments center around the planting and harvesting of crops. This makes perfect sense because the solstice and equinox positions of the sun are the most common alignments at the major sites. But other alignments oriented to the moon, planets, and stars were also intentionally fixed. These complex alignments are not functional if the goal is to plant on the same day year after year. At the end of the day, day after day, the one and only constant is the sun.

This would indicate that alignments were not just about planting. Many of the sites were already in use before the transition from nomadic hunter-gathering and herding led the tribes to planting and farming. The Irish landscape of the ancients was completely different from that of today—there were broad, pristine meadows and glens, and areas of bare rock and bogland. But, by and large, their landscape was dominated by wood and heavy forests. Trees gave way to the ax as more and more people settled, and forests suffered further with the introduction of cattle, goats, and sheep, but an environment of heavy forest puts a different spin on our interpretation of the stones that are still standing.

Standing stones and stone structures were set for all kinds of reasons. In the beginning, they served as navigational guides and marked family, clan, or tribal territories. Later, when solar and other celestial movements were recognized to be true and reliable, they became guideposts for the seasons. Their magic and simple opulence may have served that part of the human experience that leans toward the spiritual, but always with a focus on the physical sustenance of the people. To be off two or three weeks either way in planting would mean that the crops would most likely fail. Similarly, if the herds didn't make safe pastures in time for calving, or reach river crossings when they could be safely navigated, the consequences could be severe further on down the road.

> "They've come to us from pagan times and some wells, if insulted, will stop flowing and physically move to another location."
>
> —*Farmer, Corofin, Co Clare, 2001*

Beltany Stone Circle

I suggest that some of the standing stones and smaller circles represent specific alignments set by nomadic herdsmen who needed to know when to leave one area for the next in a seasonal migration. They'd stay at one place until the site alignment occurred and then they'd move on to the next. This would help explain the large number of extremely old sites and why so many of them appear to be aligned to strange or uncommon events, or possess no identifiable alignment at all. Alignments have been studied and confirmed at many sites. It would seem likely that a great number of other sites, whose care in construction is equal or superior, may well have been aligned to events we no longer recognize. A certain star rising over a point on a hill that is in line with the tip of a lone standing stone around the second week of April may mean nothing to us today, but if 4,000 or 5,000 years ago the alignment occurred a week or two before the Fergus River was known to regularly overrun it's banks, that stone was one of the most important items in a herder's bag of tricks. I believe that these people knew exactly what was going on in their world—with the sun, the moon, the stars, and planets, and how these heavenly bodies worked in accordance with the earthly rhythms of wind, water, and the changing seasons.

BELTANY STONE CIRCLe stands on a hilltop a mile or so from the village of Raphoe in County Donegal. Dating to around 3000 B.C., the shape of this circle is true, with 64 of an original 80 or more stones forming a circle 145 feet in diameter. They vary in height from four to nine feet, and one of the stones, a triangular slab just under five-feet tall, is heavily decorated with cupmarks. Also referred to as 'suncups,' these fist-sized hollows are carved on

Beltany Recumbant Stone

the inner face of the rock and indicate the presence of an alignment. There is a large outlier, standing well over six-feet tall, located some distance southeast of the circle.

Aside from its excellent condition and classic form, Beltany is best known for its astronomical alignments. At the time of this writing, as many as twenty-eight separate alignments have been attributed to this circle. These include the winter solstice sunrise, the equinoxes, the sunrise on Samain as well as a number of lunar and star alignments. More relevant to this site is a high pillar stone aligned to the cupmarked triangular slab and the sunrise on May 1, the festival of Beltane for which this circle is named.

DOTTING THE LANDSCAPE of Ireland are *fulachta fiadh*, ancient cooking sites used by nomadic groups in the years between 6000 B.C. and the time of Christ. The site was generally located at or near a spring, and the group would set up camp there and prepare their meat, usually deer or wild boar, for cooking. A trough lined with large flat stones would be filled with water, and hot stones from a nearby fire would be rolled into the trough to bring the water to a boil. The meat was then placed in the water and cooked. Afterwards, the stones were stacked together in a pile. With repeated use, the stones became brittle and surface flaking would gradually reduce their size. What remains today are kidney-shaped mounds enclosing a hollow that was the cooking trough. The flakes and small stones that occasionally had to be scooped from the trough are what actually form the mound.

A few years ago, a group of university students got together at one of the sites in an attempt to see how well this primitive process worked. What they discovered astounded them all. After filling the trough half-full of heated rocks, the water boiled for no fewer than three hours, providing more than enough heat to cook the large pig they had brought.

The term *fulachta fiadh* is thought to have come from the famous warrior bands of Ireland, the Fianna, or simply from the cooking of *fiadh*, the Irish word for deer.

THERE ARE OVER 30,000 ring forts in Ireland, 2,300 of them in County Clare alone. Of these, nearly 400 are located in the small region known as the Burren. The best known of the Burren ring forts are Cahercommane, a triple-walled cliff fort overlooking a long and narrow valley of dense hazel and rock outcroppings, and Cathair Dhuin Irghuis, a dry-stone wall masterpiece, located on the stark brow of Blackhead, about 700 feet above South Sound and Galway Bay in a place where nothing afloat in the entire Atlantic could possibly be missed.

Cahercommane sees many visitors in a year, but Cathair Dhuin Irghuis sees none but the most hardy. The majority of the other ring forts are located on private land and, with so

Clare Ring Forts

many in such a small area, a tourist can soon be satisfied with those most easily accessible. The locals, on the other hand, get nervous when tourist season comes around because they fear damage to the forts which mean so much to them. The forts in the Burren are numerous and in relatively fine shape compared to those in other parts of Ireland. This is a matter of pride among the locals and is an integral part of their identity. On the other hand, ring forts are considered vents to the Otherworld, and the locals respect that even if they repeatedly express otherwise.

> I once asked a young farm wife if she and her husband believed in fairies. Her response was not at all different from that of many others.
>
> "Oh no, not at all," she replied. "That's the old folks talking the old ways, and neither me nor my Michael believe in any of that."
>
> "But if you had a ring fort on your place," I began, "and you needed more land to run your cattle, would you consider getting a bulldozer and dozing it flat?"
>
> "A ring fort! No, not on your life," she said. "We'd never—and thank God we've not got one of those anywhere near our place—we'd never dare to be the cause of four generations of bad luck."

I was reminded of reports I'd been given by several reliable sources about a series of incidents that took place not far from there in 1999. Four men had received permission to explore a large ring fort that stood just off the highway between Ennis and the Shannon Airport. They cut down all the large ancient oaks that surrounded the fort and used a backhoe to dig up the structure. The site had been closed to the public, but I could see through the fence that it had been left in a truly sad state. The wood of the oak was gone, but the stumps had been ripped out of the ground and lay half-buried in large piles of dirt and rubble. The only thing found was the skeleton of a horse, buried there sometime around 1920. The tale was a tragedy from beginning to end. The men ran out of money and could not afford to explore further. Nor could they reclaim the site as expected; before the year was out, all four of the men were killed in strange and separate accidents along the highway between Ennis and the Shannon Airport.

A FEW MILES OUTSIDE THE VILLAGE OF KILFENORA, up a single lane and a walk across several fields is Cathair Bhaile Cinn Mhargaidh, or Caher Ballykinvarga, meaning 'fort of the head of the market.' Averaging 145 feet in diameter, the fort is an amazing structure of dressed stone walls 15-feet high and as thick as 19 feet in places. There are several large standing stones and the remains of a stone hut or two outside the fort, but most intriguing is that the fort is one of only a few in Ireland surrounded by a field of thin, pointed, waist-high stones called *chevaux de fries*, set completely around the fort for more than fifty feet, or a sling's throw from the outer wall. Obviously designed to repel enemy attacks, the stones are set upright, with slivers of sharp slate still set dangerously in between. This would impede any advance and a horse charge would have been out of the question. A narrow, sunken passage led out a gateway and through the *chevaux de fries* on the east side. The passage served

Cathair Bhaile Cinn Mhargaidh

as an entrance and exit for occupants of the fort, but its narrow, sunken design was a deadly trap for would-be assailants. It would entice the enemy to advance in a line one-at-a-time, but the way the stones were arranged along the passage forced their shield arms away from the wall. This provided a clear and open shoot for the archers defending the fort. The structure was designed for battle, and one can only image how many men died on that narrow strip.

The inside of the fort was impressive, both in size and condition. Some of the ramparts were still intact, and short rows of stones coursing the grounds appeared to be the foundations of buildings. The view from the top of the wall offered a clear panorama for a mile or more in any direction, and the local belief that a ring fort was genuine only when seven other forts were visible held true.

My suspicions were raised when I saw how tall the grasses grew inside the fort, but I soon found evidence that sheep and cattle did occasionally come inside the fort to feed. On the other hand, near the wall to the east stood one of the largest, hardiest whitethorn bushes I had ever seen. Whitethorn inside the walls of a ring fort, especially the single bush, is a sure sign of a fairy ráth. I approached the bush with caution and respect and was immediately surprised to find, though it made me feel all the more uncomfortable, the weathered skull of a horned sheep sitting neatly on a flat rock at the base of the bush. The horns were all but gone, each side still having a curl but so gnawed by rodents it was hard to tell how large they had originally been. The white of the skull had gone completely green, as if for a time it had been hidden deep among the moss and grasses that filled the fort. Sitting as it was, so neat in the sharp air and sunshine, it seemed unlikely that it had been there long. Was it a gift? An offering? Or had some tourists just recently visited the site, found the skull, and thought it might look nice sitting on the rock? At the time, the questions seemed important, relevant, the core of a true mystery. Now, with experience and reflection, I can only wonder who else besides myself was crazy enough to be out there exploring old ring forts in the coldest part of an Irish February.

HEALING WELLS were regarded as the vaginas of the earth, where flowed the water of life, and this is where the church struggled most to sever ties with the past and the power of women. The Irish, in an attempt to appease the Roman Church and still satisfy their ancient beliefs, assigned a Christian saint to each and began calling them 'holy wells.'

St. Brigid's Well, for example, is one of the most popular and well-known holy wells in Ireland and is located along the main road between Liscannor and the Cliffs of Moher in County Clare. People come here from far and wide each year on August 15 to pray, make offerings, and leave messages of thanksgiving on the walls and shelves of the small sanctuary that houses the well. In pre-Christian days the well was visited on August 1 during the Celtic festival of Lughnasa, but that date was later changed to satisfy the dictates of the church. Often referred to as 'Mary of the Gael,' St. Brigid is one of Ireland's most beloved saints. The Brigid of pre-Christian days was a daughter of the Tuatha dé Danann and was associated with poetry, healing, and smith-work. The historical Brigid lived in the sixth century and was the leader of a group of holy women who tended the 'perpetual fire' in Kildare. The group converted to Christianity under her direction and transformed the site into a Christian shrine where a succession of nuns tended the perpetual fire for many centuries afterward. Brigid is said to be buried under the same large slab as St. Patrick, on the hill overlooking the city of Downpatrick in County Down.

These holy wells, along with blessed trees and blessed bushes, were considered living things, no less living and natural than the animals in the forest or the people who came for their cure or blessing. Many tales are told about how a holy well moved, physically relocated itself after someone spoke an insult its way. There are also hole stones, slabs that have a hole carved through them that heal afflicted limbs when they are moved back and forth through the hole. Some hole stones actually have holes large enough to pass small children through.

The most common cures at holy wells are for eye problems. There are also wells which cure skin problems and arthritis. Specific rituals are particular to each and every well, and they must be performed precisely if the cures are to work. One set may be as simple as reciting a 'Hail Mary' while walking 'round a well clockwise four times. Another can be as complex as doing a seven-round recital of specific prayers every Monday for seven weeks, reversing the direction of the round every other week. Each well is different and a person is normally required to find the keeper of the well in order to learn the particular rituals associated with it. The position of well keeper is usually hereditary, a member of a specific family inheriting the task from one in the previous generation. These people are required to know the rituals, the history, and any tales associated with the well. They are also responsible for the overall upkeep and repair of the site. There are families in Ireland who legitimately claim they've been the keepers of a certain well for many hundreds, if not thousands, of years.

Some wells cannot be visited directly because a keeper, usually a woman, must physically bring the water to the afflicted. There is such a well in County Donegal. The waters from this well are said to heal all kinds of ailments, from poor eyesight to soreness in the limbs and joints. Unfortunately, the woman who had served the community as the keeper died and the community had been, at the time of my visit, nearly a year without someone to carry the

Brigid's Well

St. Patrick's Grave

Brigid's Cross

Hole Stone

Holy Well, Corofin

waters to the ill. When I asked what would happen, I was told that the situation was extremely delicate and completely out of human hands. Only the *sídhe* could appoint a keeper for this particular well. This well had never been associated with saints or other Christian virtues. It was ancient—pre-Christian, believed to be pre-Pagan, and went back much further than anyone could say. All anyone knew for certain was that this well was still there for the people of the community, and although some were growing anxious about the amount of time that had passed, they understood that when the powers of the place decided it was time, some woman of the community would find herself at the well and know that she had been given the responsibility of serving the people for the rest of her life.

Glouthane Standing Stone

Glouthane Stone Circle

I GOT UP EARLY, well before dawn, so that I could reach the circle in the fog and mist. My reasons for this were practical ones—special film plus special weather conditions often resulted in extra-special effects.

I found the road, the parking spot near the broken gate beside the large tree, and started walking up the hill the 200 or so yards the guidebook gave as the distance. I walked and walked, thinking that the fog made a few hundred yards seem like forever. The mist shrouded, yawned, and floated, and finally I reached the ridge.

Burren Wall and Storm

I walked back and forth along the ridge, looking for a large circle whose stones stood well over seven-feet high. I reached what I sensed was the highest spot and started to spiral downward. I climbed over a stone fence and started across a field when out of the fog came a snort and a grunt followed by the ominous shape of a huge bull. I remember little about what happened those next few moments, but I do recall darting and dodging and finally clearing the fence. A roar approached from the mist and I thought it might actually be the sound of my own death. A wind struck me so that I was turned around to face the valley. The fog had lifted and, before me, though perhaps a mile or more away, two dogs were herding a rolling mass of white over a ridge and down a dark slope toward a man leaning against a car yet another ridge away. I laughed and sucked in as much air as my lungs would take. You may not always find what you're looking for in Ireland, but the powers that be will sometimes provide all the special effects you need.

White Bull

Parknabinnia Wedgetomb

Only the Hardy

Connemara Country House

Hill of Tara

By the Hand of Macha

Teamhair is the ancient name given the Hill of Tara. One of the most religious and revered sites in all of Ireland, it was from this hill that the *ard rí*, the High Kings of Ireland, ruled the land. The place was sometimes called Druim Caín, the 'beautiful ridge,' or Druim na Descan, the 'ridge of the outlook.' When walking the path that leads to the top of the hill today, one can easily appreciate why. The long gradual slope eventually flattens at the top for an amazing view of the broad plains in the Boyne and Blackwater valleys below. All that remains of the complex is a series of grass-covered mounds and earthworks that say little about the 5,000 years of habitation this hill has seen.

Just north of the Mound of Hostages, a small passage grave dating to around 2500 B.C., is a large rectangular earthwork that once supported the Great Banquet Hall. Known in Irish as the Teach Miodhchuarta, or 'house of mead-circling,' the structure measured 90-feet wide by 755-feet long and was built to serve thousands of guests during times of feast and celebration. Tradition also suggests that the Great Hall housed all the leading knights of Ireland, acted as the ceremonial entrance to Tara, and was the point where all the major roads of ancient Ireland converged.

South of the Mound of Hostages is the King's Ráth and Royal Seat. In its center stands the Lia Fáil or 'Stone of Destiny.' Clearly phallic in design and form, the stone is said to be one of the four treasures brought to Ireland by the Tuatha dé Danann, a gift from the gods that would roar three times when he who would be rightful king stood upon it. Although the stone has been moved several times, it originally stood beside the Mound of Hostages. The chamber of the mound is specifically aligned to catch the sun at the time of two major Celtic festivals: Samain or 'Summer's End,' on November 1 and Imbolc, or 'The Budding,' in early February.

"The Hill of Tara is one of the main reasons this county is still referred to as 'Royal Meath.' It's just so old, and it seems to have played a part in everything we understand about Ireland."

—*Owner of a B&B, Slane, Co Meath, 2002*

Lia Fáil, Hill of Tara

A great fair or *feis*, was held at Tara at the time of Samain. Lasting three days before and three days after, the *feis* was an intricate affair, much more than just a week of festive celebration. Here, the ancient laws were recited and defined, new laws were enacted, grievances were acknowledged, and disputes were settled. As was customary at all such assemblies, the ancient history was recited before all the people by the king's *seanachie*, or storyteller, while the many other *seanachie* carefully monitored his every word. The storyteller could not distort or modify the accounts in the slightest, lest he be subjected to public criticism and humiliation by his highly-accomplished and disciplined associates. This extremely efficient method of confirming and conveying the country's history as a carefully monitored oral tradition was practiced for many thousands of years before the introduction of writing. Even then, the practice did not die. Often hidden behind the veil of folklore, it continued on for many long centuries in response to a Christian church bent on revising what it considered a sinful, pagan past. Hence, the rich history described by Yeats and Lady Gregory was theirs to record only because of people so dedicated as to pass the words on generation by generation, mouth by mouth.

There are so many stories associated with Tara that the difference between fact and fable is all but impossible to distinguish. The kings, for example, may have been the most influential men in the land, but it is doubtful that the kings of Tara ever had complete political control over Ireland. The term 'High Kings' was more symbolic than exact and, except for specific periods between A.D. 400 and 1022, it is a matter of record that Tara was obliged to share power with countless other regional kings and clan chieftains.

Nevertheless, Tara remains the royal seat of romance and enchantment for the Irish. It was here that the great goddess Queen Medb first employed her mystical powers and a vast host of druids to reign over the land. Her ráth, some 750-feet in diameter, lies a half-mile to the south of Tara Hill. The young Fionn mac Cumhaill accomplished his first heroic act by killing the evil Aillén mac Midgna, a fairy musician who lulled the people of Tara to sleep and then burned the structure to the ground every Samain for twenty-three years. Tradition holds that Patrick lit a paschal (Easter) fire on the Hill of Slane in A.D. 433 as an act of rebellion against Lóegaire, High King of Ireland, who decreed that no fire should be lit within sight of the Hill of Tara. Patrick's act symbolized Christ's triumph over paganism and, although Lóegaire was furious, he sought to meet with Patrick and question him. During the encounter, Patrick killed one of the king's druids and summoned an earthquake to subdue the king's guards. He then used the three-leaved shamrock to explain the concept of the Holy Trinity to the king and his court. Lóegaire made peace with Patrick and, although he never converted, the king allowed Patrick to continue his evangelizing. On the eve of Easter Sunday, the local parish priest still lights a bonfire on the Hill of Slane and the shamrock remains the national symbol of Ireland.

Although the High Kings of Tara were normally buried at Brug na Bóinne or Newgrange, just to the south of the Royal Seat are the remains of the Ráth of King Lóegaire. Here the king is said to be buried fully armed in an upright position in order to see any approaching enemies of Ireland. To the north of the Royal Seat are numerous other mounds and earthworks. One of them, as legends go, could be the very place where the head and hand of Cúchulainn were buried following his death at Sliab Fúait. Then again, these two elements of the ancient past may instead be found at Emain Macha to the North near Armagh.

IF TARA IS IRELAND'S ROYAL SEAT, Emain Macha is certainly its Camelot. As England had Arthur and his Knights of the Round Table, so did this large hill of broken trenches and mounds act as headquarters for the Kings of Ulster and their famed Knights of the Red Branch. Cúchulainn was their greatest champion and, according to the men of Ulster, it was here and not Tara that his earthly remains are buried.

Known also as Navan Fort, excavations indicate that the site was in use prior to 3000 B.C., but the hill's rise to splendor did not commence until around 700 B.C. when construction on the round house was begun. It is believed that Emain Macha is the same place the Greek geographer Ptolemy called Isamnion in the second century A.D. The discovery on site of the skull of a Barbary ape indicates that the location was known well outside the confines of Ireland. The hill fort was burned and abandoned around the fourth or fifth century A.D., but continued to be the site of an annual *feis* similar to those at Tara, Tailtiu, and Cruachain through late medieval times.

One legend tells how a Queen named Macha Mong Ruadh or 'red haired' had her husband build the residence in her honor. She marked out the area with a brooch (eó) she wore about her neck (muin), and from then on the hill was called Eó-muin Macha, or 'neck brooch of Macha.' She also lends her name to the hill-town of Armagh, or Ard Macha, which means 'height of Macha.'

The more popular legend, and what, for me, is one of the most marvelous and heartrending of all Irish sagas, tells how Macha, a woman of the Tuatha dé Danann, married and became pregnant by a wealthy, widowed landowner. He decided to attend the annual fair and horse race and, against her warnings not to mention her name, he bragged that she could beat the best of the king's chariots in a footrace. The king, stung by these words, had the husband seized and the woman delivered to him. She cried out to be released because she was pregnant and near her time, but was told to run or see her child die. She shouted

Emain Macha

that her name was Macha and that a great evil would fall upon the men of Ulster because of the affair. She won the race with ease but, as she crossed the finish line, she doubled over in pain and gave birth to twins: a girl and a boy. From that day on the place was known as Emain Macha or 'the twins of Macha.' Because of her humiliation and birth pains, the men of Ulster were cursed to suffer the debilitating pangs of childbirth for nine-times-nine generations whenever they found themselves in great difficulty. The only people exempt were women, young boys, and Cúchulainn, because he was a son of the Tuatha dé Danann.

Accounts vary as to what happened next. Some say that Macha died immediately after giving birth. Others say she went back to her people, to the *sídhe* and the Otherworld, to join Nemain and Badb as one of the three war goddesses that make up the persona, the Mórrígan. As for the men of Ulster, they were said to suffer indeed and, because they were so often overcome with birth pains when in battle, Cúchulainn was left to defend Ulster alone.

The circular mound resembled a crown one fine day in April when I first took the long sloping path to the top of Emain Macha. The weather had been cold and wet for two weeks prior, but that day, a Sunday, was as bright and warm as only the best spring days can be in Ireland. Consequently, the hill was crawling with people and it seemed like fully half the population of County Armagh were there. They were hiking, picnicking, or dozing comfortably on the soft, grassy slopes of the central mound and, as if to add insult to injury, someone had a Manchester United match blaring loudly in the background.

I couldn't honestly begrudge or blame them for enjoying the day, but I was confronted by a dilemma. Should I photograph the hill with people in the scene, or spend the next several hours trying to catch a deserted frame here and there as people moved in and out of the shot? As I considered these possibilities, the circumstances changed entirely and I had little choice but to adjust as best I could.

In a matter of moments, a wind began and heavy, dark clouds blew in from behind the mound. I moved toward the ring of huge oaks that surrounded the mound, fastened the cover on the camera bag securely, slipped the hood of my waterproof parka over my head, and threw my back to the gale. The wind picked up at an ever-increasing rate and the sky exploded in drenching sheets of rain. People were shrieking and screaming off the mound and down the hill. I stood there thinking how quickly everything had changed, and how strange it was that a storm could rage so from my rear while I and the valley below were still exposed to bright sunshine. A large branch flew by and the gusting volume of rain changed direction, from left to right and back again, every few seconds or so. I hunkered under my fabric shell, occasionally closing my eyes tight as the gale slapped my face with a blast of ice-cold fury. Just as I thought the craziness was letting up, the torrent surged even more and the light became incredible. Before me were all the colors of the spectrum, not as lines or arches, but as the tiniest flashing pinpoints, swirling and dancing in a radiance that seemed to emanate from the ground itself. The gale screamed and roared and I thought back to Shakespeare's Lear. I screamed and roared right back, it thrilled me so. I sang and laughed until I felt I was about to fall,

and that's when she touched me . . .

Emain Macha Moat

with the most gentle whiff of airborne mist, unexpectedly warm and sweet. My right cheek was embraced and lightly stroked as if by the hand of one completely and wholly female. I was calmed and excited at the same time, impassioned by a purity of affection that carried through to my soul. I inhaled, breathed in the essence, and at once knew. I was welcome. I was cherished. I was a part of this wildness and understood that everything—not just the moment, or the day, or the project at hand—was leading me down a path that was extraordinary.

I was left blinking in fascination as the storm subsided around me. Just as quickly as it had started, the rain stopped, the wind died, and the sun returned to the other side of the hill. What had happened, though far from expected, struck me as not-at-all surprising. I casually picked up my cameras and set my sights to the task at hand. I was the only person left on the mountain. The mound was mine, for an hour or so at least, to photograph however I chose.

Later that evening on the drive back to Belfast, the news began with the 'rogue' storm that had raged across the hills near Armagh. It reported damages, a few injuries, and how scores of people were driven off the hill at Navan Fort. I smiled over the fury and remembered the hand on my cheek. How strange it sometimes seems when the strangest things don't seem very strange at all.

From the Burren

Blight on the Emerald Isle

SPRINGTIME IN IRELAND is an amazing season, but the spring of 2001 was overshadowed by the foot and mouth crisis and everyone, from the ordinary shop owner in Dublin to the farmer struggling in the most isolated corner of the land, possessed a clear edge of concern. The Cooley Peninsula was silent, "dead" the old-timers called it, due to the culling of over 50,000 sheep and cattle. In the Burren, however, we had lambs jumping and calves bawling and for the first time in a long time, Galway Bay was as smooth as glass as I drove toward Doolin from Bell Harbor.

It was a bright sunny day and I used the time in good fashion, photographing the amazing display of wildflowers suddenly busting out all over the Burren. The Burren is an amazing expanse of limestone cliffs and plateaus in northwest County Clare. Lacking the lush greens Ireland is so famous for, the grey limestone pavements often shock the first-time visitor with their severity and starkness. But the Burren is far from just the 'stony place' its ancient name implies and a closer look reveals a landscape full of life and vitality.

This small area is home to more than 600 different species of flowering plants, ferns, and trees, fully one-half of the native flora in all of Ireland. From the fissures and deep crevices grow an amazing assortment of wildflowers, with Arctic, Alpine, and Mediterranean plants blooming in profusion side by side. Some of these are particular to this environment alone, especially the variety of colorful orchids considered so rare elsewhere. Fox, badger, and many other mammal species range freely, as do large herds of wild and troublesome feral goats. The bird life is astounding and nothing else compares to the magic and majesty of their song on a warm spring day.

There are several varieties of orchids growing in the Burren, and they bloom with little overlap at different times throughout spring and summer. They may be much smaller than

"I say where Ireland is, and I'm tellin' you you'll not get to Ireland until you put your feet in that bloody trough [of disinfectant] and step through the door."

—*An immigration officer to a reluctant French couple at Shannon Airport, 2001*

Early Purple Orchid

their tropical cousins, but what they lack in size is compensated for by sheer numbers. The Early Purple Orchid, *Orchis mascula*, is a stunningly beautiful plant and is much a part of Irish legend and folklore. Said to have grown at the foot of the Cross, the leaves typically appear spattered with dark purple-black spots, memory of the blood of Christ. More significant than this, however, is how the name translates and what uses the Irish have made of the plant.

The Irish name for the Early Purple Orchid is, *magairlin meidhreach*, or 'large testicle.' The bulbs of the plant occur in pairs and so resemble that particular part of the male anatomy. The Irish chose to call it after the root despite the beauty of the flower. Likewise, the wordsmiths of Latin chose the word *orchis* or *orchid*, which also means 'testicles.' In several places of Ireland, but especially in the Burren, this observation led to the use of orchids as a main ingredient in love potions, particularly those designed to enhance the affections of the male. I can still recall my mother telling me how her granny often spoke of the potions available in the old country to young women in want of a man, and how they were made from the roots of magical plants and flowers.

Fortunately for the survival of this species, the effect works only in combination with words spoken by someone having the *piseog*, the ability to cast spells, so the plant has not been harvested to extinction by people mistaking it for an aphrodisiac. Equally remarkable is how the plant's connection with Christ is wedded to a past undoubtedly much, much older than Christianity. Those wise in the ways of the ancient arts would have appreciated the orchid for itself alone, but with the coming of Christ, whether they considered him the Son of God, or a son of the many, the spattering of leaves at the foot of the cross would have only confirmed the magical properties of the plant. Then again, the wedding may have merely been a way to continue on with an old and wonderful tradition while avoiding condemnation by the Catholic Church.

NEWS PROGRAMS transmitted over the radio in the spring of 2001 offered the listener an emotional roller-coaster ride whose destination lay somewhere between salvation and absolute doom. One story would talk about how Ireland was still the fastest growing economy on the planet, with significant wage increases expected in the coming months, and the next

Stone Fence, The Burren

would explain how the foot and mouth scare had adversely affected just about every aspect of Irish society. Tourism was down, way down, and agriculture paid a heavy price between the culls and restrictions that forbade farmers to sell their crop of spring calves and lambs. This became an added expense for the farmers, as they had to feed stock that should have gone to market weeks earlier. In the Burren, the situation was even more severe.

The topography of the region makes the Burren a great source of winter grass and herding has been the main occupation there for nearly 5,000 years. No one can say with confidence when the stone fences considered so wonderfully Irish today were first laid, but it is understood to have been long ago with people who needed to move cattle from one location to another through the vast forests that once dominated this landscape. Indeed, the Irish word for a road, *bohreen*, literally means 'where cattle pass.' The fences may have also served as boundaries for clan or family territories. Whatever their considerations may have been, these people came up with a remarkably efficient way to control the movement of large herds of hearty beasts when manpower was limited and the terrain was unsuited for herding with horses.

Stone Fence and Road above Fanor

Stone fences are found all over Ireland, but those that snake and course their way across the Burren are like no other—not in Ireland and perhaps not like fences found anywhere else in the world. Built of limestone pavements, the stones are long, relatively thin rectangles set upright instead of flat on the ground. When you look at them broadside, especially on a backlit ridge where light shows through, they resemble a net and the stones, placed as they are end-on-end, appear to mesh much like the nets they resemble. When I asked why the stones were set this way, I was more often than not told it's just the way they've always been done. Nevertheless, time and the elements have proven this method stronger than any other. The net-like mesh created by the vertical stacking allows the harshest of winds to pass through while animals can't easily push them over. I've also been told that not everyone can build them, that it does require a special talent, but, whether set fresh by a craftsman or made right again by replacing a fallen stone or two, the walls are clearly the source of much pride among the people. No one is sure how old they really are; they've just always been there. As surely as they are part of the identity of the people of the Burren, there are certain customs that are at least as old and important as the great stone fences.

The mild climate of Ireland allows for a ten-month growing season. Grasses grow from mid-February to late December, providing enough grass in the hills for grazing cattle throughout the winter without need of silage. Normal procedure would have the cattle moving out of the Burren and into the valleys by mid-March. Unfortunately, the foot and mouth restrictions would not allow the normal movements and, by the first of May, most of the fields were severely overgrazed. Farmers were forced to spend extra money on silage and it was doubtful that the Burren grasses would recover by October when the cattle would normally return for their winter grazing. Knowledge about the way things work, procedures and processes that have kept this tiny piece of the planet healthy and productive from generation to generation for 5,000 years were suddenly disrupted. Thoughts I'd had the first day of my

Rows of Stone Fences

An Easy Sunday Morning

Sammy Glenn's Butcher Shop

three-month stay about the Irish, their well-earned fortune with the Celtic Tiger and how it seemed there was always another tragedy just around the corner, appeared to be a cruel joke on everyone.

In a world where corporate agribusiness threatens to genetically alter entire species of livestock with artificial hormones and synthetic compounds, the Irish struggle to maintain what has long been considered the sturdiest and healthiest herds of livestock in all of Europe. The resurgence of old diseases seems less threatening as new, far more potent diseases emerge. The sudden appearance of mad cow disease and, more recently, the foot and mouth crisis, are now being blamed on an agribusiness that is both inconsistent and neglectful. Millions of cattle and sheep were culled and burned in England—and this in spite of their own recommendations against burning infected carcasses. Foot and mouth is an airborne virus and extensive research conducted in England during a similar outbreak in the 1960s suggests that burning can create circumstances that actually spread the disease. The few confirmed cases of foot and mouth disease found in the Republic of Ireland in 2001 led to the slaughter of 50,000 sheep and cattle on the Cooley Peninsula, but the Irish followed the recommendations of the research, burying the carcasses in pits and then covering them with lime. The disease was stopped and no further cases surfaced. While agribusiness is currently building artificial landscapes in multi-story factory buildings designed to house thousands of animals on the continent, most markets in Ireland still display the names of the family-owned farms

Burren Bull

which supply the meat in the cases on a particular day. Farmers still swear to having goats or a donkey in with the stock, and limit the numbers of cattle on the land—not because it presents an overgrazing problem, but because they understand that too many cattle in a limited area produce catastrophes like mad cow and the foot and mouth disease.

The history of Ireland is the history of cattle. Men were herding cattle on the landscape of Ireland more than 6,000 years ago. Unfortunately, farming is affected by market prices even more than other industries, and times get harder as costs go up. On the other hand, more and more people in Ireland and on the continent are spending in favor of organically-grown products. They are willing to pay the extra cost for the guarantee and, with Ireland exporting nearly eighty percent of what it produces, there is certainly some hope for the future of agriculture in Ireland.

Cow & Storm

Burren Feral Goat

Burren Country House

Quin Abbey

Poulawack Cemetary Cairn

Mullach Mor

Links to the Ancients

T HE TRANSITION FROM THE OLD BELIEFS TO CHRISTIANITY was not a great leap for the Irish. Cúchulainn, Brigid, and so many others were believed to be the offspring of gods and men so it was easy for them to accept that Christ was born the Son of God and a mortal woman. Likewise, the resurrection of Christ was not at all hard to believe because the Tuatha dé Danann themselves could die and live again. The transition, though not always orderly, was quite understandable: shaman to druid to priest; Danu, the Mother Goddess, to Medb, to Brigid and the Virgin Mary. The Church created new links or remodeled older precepts in order to win over the Irish. Cúchulainn was not in conflict with Christ anymore than Medb was at odds with the Virgin. The new was tied fast to the old. A past of magic and myth acted only to strengthen the newer faith.

THE SCENE IS RUSTIC, rural, classic Ireland. In the background is an old abbey. Once a strong and sturdy house of faith, it is now abandoned and crumbling, little more than a windbreak for the sheep and cattle that graze in the surrounding fields. To one side is an old cemetery in which stands a Celtic High Cross from the early ninth century. Carved into its stone are simple crosses, crucifixes, and other Christian symbols, but the vast majority of the cross is covered with an intricate pattern of knots, spirals, and other designs of a highly stylized Celtic form. The cross is said to have taken two monks over thirty-five years to complete and clearly their Irish soul and not their attachment to the Holy Roman Church came through the stone.

At the base of the cross, just to the right near the grass and blooming daffodils, is a stone basin. Old and partially broken, it was shaped from a piece of granite centuries ago. Some folks say the basins were made for holy water, Ireland's earliest baptismal fonts. Others claim

"The fairies possess a special power called *féth fíada*, a mist or veil that makes them invisible or allows them to take on the form of an animal. This power was given by them to Ireland's saints, and Patrick himself used it to take on the form of a deer while on his way to Christianize Tara."

—*A* seanachie, *Co Cork, 2002*

opposite:
High Cross & Abbey

The Bishop, Kilfenora Cathedral

they were fashioned to serve as watering basins for wrens—small, energetic birds believed to be the earthly attendants of Medb, Queen of the Otherworld. The basins are scattered all over Ireland—in fields, cemeteries, on hilltops, occasionally near stone circles, but almost always in or around old abandoned churches and abbeys. Those who believe they were made for wrens say Medb is so honored simply because she was a goddess. She was never Christian, but, "At the end of the day," as they say, "she was one of 'Them' just the same." As with Jesus and Mary, Medb is of the divine, and the stone basins serve as a link between Christian Ireland and the Land of Ever-Young.

Virgin of Quin

OVER THE DOORWAY of the old church in the village of Kilnaboy is the carved relief of a Sheela-na-gig, a pre-Christian image of a woman exposing her genitalia. No satisfactory explanation has ever been provided as to origin, date, or reason why these images were placed on churches, but the vast majority—seventy-five of less than a hundred worldwide—are found in Ireland. Some believe that the Sheela is a fertility symbol from pagan times that served as a cure for barrenness. Others say they are set over the main entrances to ward off evil. Still others suggest that they are reminders of the ancient earth goddess whose rule over life and death predated Christ and the changes his life and death brought. Whatever their true purpose, Sheela-na-gigs go way back in time and clearly represent a link between Christian and much older beliefs.

After shooting several photos of the Sheela at Kilnaboy, I wandered among the tombstones that surround the roofless walls of the old stone church. Because Ireland is a place of limited land and long habitation, graveyards are made up of small family plots which are used again and again to bury the departed members of the family. My exploring proved a bit disconcerting, however, due to the number of bones visible in the soil and on the surface of many of the graves. Along with finger and toe bones, there were teeth, vertebrae, and odd pieces of jawbone. More distressing was the realization that, while some of the teeth I examined showed wear, none showed decay and, indeed, those in the grave seemed to be in much better condition than many of those found in my own mouth. The assessment took me back to a book I once read about the lack of dental problems among people living on totally natural, native diets. Interestingly enough, western Clare had been one of the test locations for that study, completed sometime in the early 1950s, and the evidence scattered about the graveyard seemed to support the findings.

Sheela-na-gig

Conversations afterwards with locals revealed that professional gravediggers are rare in Ireland, especially in the countryside where it is still customary for a group of men from the community to dig the grave. To be called upon by the family of the deceased is considered an honor and the digging actually becomes something of a festive get-together, complete with food and drink. The gravediggers I've spoken with all agree that leaving bones lying around as described above is not the way graves are meant to be. They also agree that missing a bone or two is easy, especially in old graveyards where the plots have been used and reused numerous times. The established procedure allows for a grave to be reused after ten years. The men dig down and remove whatever is left of the old casket. The bones are then collected, placed in cloth or paper sacks, and stacked around the new casket before filling in the grave. By collecting and burying the bones together in one grave, the lives of all the preceding generations of a family are blended in the same hollow of earth. This practice is not all that different from that of the ancient days when the ash that remained after a cremation was mixed together with the ash in the clan or tribal urn.

Corcomroe Abbey

Altar, Corcomroe Abbey

Quin Abbey Interior

Kilmacduagh Monestary

*Kilfenora Cathedral
Windows*

Penitential Cairn

O'Brien's Tomb, Corcomroe Abbey

High Cross, Kells

ALL TOO OFTEN the legends and mythological tales of a people are perceived to be the products of romantic invention, misconception, or ignorance and are, at best, exaggerations of half-truths designed to entertain inquisitive children and superstitious fools. Such stories are assumed to be stretched way out of proportion by time, no longer fitting the realities of the world we understand. However, I have discovered that Irish tales from antiquity are not as far-fetched as might be expected.

The Battle for the White Strand is an ancient tale of courage, honor, and extraordinary violence. The list of combatants is long and impressive, a kind of who's who of the third century A.D. The battle lasted a year and one day, and was fought between the Enemies of Ireland, led by Dáire Donn, High King of the Great World, and Ireland's Fionn mac Cumhaill and his heroic band of warriors, the Fianna Éireann. Both sides suffered heavy losses and the Fianna were all but wiped out, but Fionn and a few survivors, aided by the Tuatha dé Danann, eventually rallied and drove the invaders out of Ireland. They became the greatest warriors Ireland has ever known and their stories make up a completely separate heroic period in Irish literature called the Fenian Cycle.

The White Strand lies in a broad bay of sand beaches on the Dingle Peninsula in the southwest of Ireland. The beach seems almost level, with a fine, cream-white sand that forms a smooth, firm base just right for walking, playing sports or, in this case, waging battle. Except for power lines, asphalt, and a few buildings, the strand is exactly as described in the old tales. Fionn's headquarters, an ancient fort overlooking the bay, is still there although it stands in disrepair. There are the familiar sounds of wind and wave and an array of song and sea birds creates an atmosphere of peace and harmony. The real events that the White Strand suffered those many centuries ago have been lost to time and a legend whose scope and drama is hard to accept—a lengthy, complex, and fantastic tale.

White Strand

Cúchulainn's Leap

Nevertheless, Ireland is blessed with many such places and Cúchulainn's Leap is one that proved to be much more interesting in reality than I had ever imagined. The legend tells how a Hag named Mal was chasing the great warrior, Cúchulainn, all over Ireland in an attempt to win his love. He was terrified at the prospect and, when she finally cornered him on a narrow, sheer-sided spit of headland at the very southern tip of County Clare, he leapt onto a nearby sea stack and she fell to her death when she tried to follow. The sea turned red with her blood and her body washed up at several points along the coast. Hag's Head near the Cliffs of Moher and Milltown Malbay near Spanish Point are two such places that still bear her name.

I drove to the end of the headland and parked the car just outside the gate of Loophead Lighthouse. Loop is an anglicized version of the word leap and this has become the name for Cúchulainn's Leap. I fully expected the size of the sea stack and its distance from the head-land to be something truly fantastic, so that Cúchulainn's great feat might actually rival the

Hag's Head

opposite:
Sea Pinks at Loophead Lighthouse

tall tales told about the American giant Paul Bunyan and his famous blue ox. What surprised me, however, was how the sea stack stood level with the headland and the distance between them was such that an athlete in good physical condition could indeed make such a leap. The distance from the top of the headland and sea stack to the water is nearly 700 feet, certainly a depth worth consideration, but the gap between the cliff tops is well within the range of human capability.

Before writing reached the Emerald Isle, the time-honored tradition was to orally pass on the stories that made up the past as accurately as possible. The *seanachie*, or storytellers, checked each other word-by-word and would disgrace anyone who intentionally tried to alter the makeup of a tale. Amateur archeologists trusting that tradition scanned the sands of the White Strand with metal detectors in the early 1960s and uncovered broken swords, shields, and chariot parts in such numbers that serious historians were forced to take notice. As for Cúchulainn's famous feat, someone with a calm resolve built a small stone cairn on the sea stack as evidence that just about anything is possible in Ireland.

WHAT MAGNIFICENCE . . . .

Irish dogs and Irish horses and how both have been bred to suit the landscape and people with as much success and satisfaction as anywhere else on earth. Dogs arrived with the first humans nearly 9,000 years ago and have played a major role in the culture ever since. The giant hunting hounds so loved and admired by Fionn and the Fianna took on a persona just short of the gods and, while they may have been the first to gain such recognition, the status of dogs, especially among the working breeds, has changed little since.

Living three months on a dairy farm taught me much about the relationship between a man and his dogs. They are companions and workmates and rarely will you find a farmer working without a dog about. On the farm especially, they are not treated as pets. Most of them sleep with the stock or in places outside the house. They may be praised or punished, but are not to be babied or fussed over because a dog which becomes too independent may become a threat to the stock. More often than not, they are treated as children in training. Dogs have certain tasks to perform and the day-to-day efficiency of the operation often depends on how quickly they learn and how well they retain that knowledge. They love to work and, like all dogs, they'll seize any opportunity to play, but they are always absolutely tuned to the temperament of their human masters.

I was so often amazed at how really sharp the dogs can be and how smoothly they fit into the rhythms of the farm. I have seen farmers whistle and point toward fields on faraway hills. The dogs run off and twenty minutes later return with sixty or more head of cattle ready for milking. I've been to informal competitions where dogs were herding and the bets were flying, and I've spent more than one Sunday afternoon in a pub trying to muster the same enthusiasm as the farmers around me for watching dog trials on TV.

Once while talking to a farmer, I watched an old arthritic black and white collie-cross teaching one of his own the ways of their world. Without any visible coaching from the farmer, the older dog 'told' the younger to get after the cattle, and when the younger over-stepped his bounds, the older 'told' him to back off. There was a communication going on between them that I found hard to believe, but when I mentioned it to the farmer, he simply smiled in their direction and said, "Yep, the pup's got real potential."

IRELAND'S HORSES are loved and revered on a par with its dogs, and I've heard it said more than a few times that Ireland has more horseflesh per square kilometer than any other country in Europe. Just about every farm has one, and if a farm doesn't, the people there would probably like one. Rarely a weekend goes by that there isn't a horse fair somewhere within easy driving distance. Even in the brick-enclosed neighborhoods of Dublin, horses are still kept and occasionally break out of their backyard stalls to create traffic problems on the narrow streets of the city. Horse racing is a sport whose season runs from October through April, and just about everyone in the country will spend a day or two at the track.

Thoroughbreds and quarter horses are admired for their speed and grace but the Connemara Pony, though it stands just a hand short of being a horse, is one of the most hardy, dependable breeds Ireland has ever seen. Bred for the rocky, wind-blown boglands of the Connemara Peninsula, they are heavy-boned and muscular, the kind of animal warriors and

opposite:
Road to Loophead

85

Burren Pony

long-riders found ideal. The Connemara takes readily to the sea, often swimming between islands to graze. The beast is truly Irish in invention and the centuries have seen them spread throughout the island and, recently, to Europe and the Americas.

I was not at all surprised to find two very pregnant Connemara mares feeding in a rocky field in the Burren of County Clare. Disbelief over their size forced me to stop the car, they were so great with foal. Like the cattle and sheep, they could not be moved because of the foot and mouth crisis, so they were stuck in the wind-blown highlands until the restrictions allowed them to be returned to the safety and shelter of a stable.

I walked up to the stone fence that stood between us and was about to set the camera on the top of one of the stones when off to my left came a scream and a snort and the charging form of one of the most magnificent creatures I have ever seen. The muddy-white stallion came on with the madness and abandon of a wild Montana mustang. Twice he slammed into the fence, nostrils flared and snorting, his ears laid back so firmly they disappeared in the massive mane that cloaked his face and head. He pawed and shrieked and made it clear the mares were his.

I was caught completely off-guard, and found myself a bit surprised that in my amazement and fascination I had not taken so much as a single step backward. I was standing fewer than two arms length from the wall and, when next the stallion blew, foam and a rush of air hit my face.

Perhaps it was the wildness of it all, or the kind of madness that comes over those living in wild places too long alone, but I was without fear when I decided to move even closer. We faced each other, and after a few words of reassurance regarding my intentions with the mares, I drew a long, deep breath and blew a blast of air his way. He stopped pawing but shook his head as if my breath were foreign. Remembering a trick I had learned from a horse trainer in Montana, I leaned in close, actually dodging once as he swung his head, and gently breathed into his open nostrils. He snorted and stiffened, but after another breath, he settled down completely. He would not let me touch him, on that point he was clear, but for the moment he appeared at ease with my voice and words.

As I spoke to him, I was impressed by his power and strength. His body was magnificent, and his long mane blew wildly in the breeze. I photographed him frame after frame, this way and that, taking plenty of time and using several different kinds of film. I was determined to record the moment and his spirit as clearly as possible. He truly exhibited interest, becoming playful and mischievous to the point that he appeared to be posing. We worked together for twenty minutes or so, until he bobbed his head a few times, made the softest, strangest sound, and walked casually to the other side of the field.

Some would say he had the devil in him, that he'd gone mad with lust and land and wind. If that were true, then I had gone completely mad as well. He and I understood each other. We communicated. We exchanged thoughts and spoke in that wordless, soundless language reserved for those who use their 'other' senses to converse. Wildness. Madness. Magic. One is the same as the others and the devil was nowhere to be seen.

Co Clare

Tales from the Bright Side

I'D SPENT MOST OF A DAY driving around the countryside in search of Carrigagulla, a stone circle which, according to the guidebook, was in exceptionally fine condition and in an "easy-to-find" location near the southern coast of County Cork. More and more, I was learning the subtle truths about guidebooks and when I finally admitted that I was completely confused and disoriented by the directions, I threw the guidebook into the rear seat and sought out a farmhouse with the hope that I might find someone who knew the circle's location.

While many people would think this a completely logical thing to do, I must say that this practice, asking the locals for directions, can more often than not leave one all the more confused and frustrated. With so many stone circles in Ireland, asking someone where a particular stone circle is can lead to, "Ach friend, which one are ye lookin' for?"

"Well, the guidebook only mentions one."

"Well, there's one on that hill over there, another in that field behind ye, one just the other side of that hedge, and there's two more just downstream from that *fulachta fiadh* that sits just to the right of that spring."

The danger is that when you ask, they give you far more information than you expected and, although you might spend the entire day exploring some of the most amazing structures in antiquity, you may never locate the actual site you had so needed to document and photograph.

Then, too, there are so many secondary roads in Ireland the likelihood of getting the right one is slim, especially when directions are typically, "Take the third right past the field that has the black and white cows in it, not the one with the bulls and white cattle—the wee field just past the second white house on the left is the one—and then you turn and go on for a

opposite:
Where the Fairies Live

91

Carrigagulla Stone Circle

time until you get to a stand of short trees with one big tree at the end, those being real short with the one tall, . . ." and the man is talking so fast that he hasn't stopped long enough to breathe and he ends it all with, ". . . just up the road, like, it's there, and a walk up the hill."

Often, one finds it hard to believe that the people of this land are not intentionally trying to be confusing. They know exactly where things are and if they don't, they'll more than likely invite you in for tea while they make a phone call or two. The Irish are undoubtedly the most genuine, helpful, and hospitable people I have ever had the pleasure to encounter. On the other hand, they often leave one far more confused by getting overly excited at the prospect of having an opportunity to put some poor, lost Yank back on track.

In any event, I spotted the farmer immediately upon entering the narrow drive—a short burly man covered in mud and manure and working so hard at digging that steam was actually rising from his body in the cold damp air. He walked over to the car and I greeted him with, "I may well be lost, but at least I'm seeing the best of what Ireland's got to offer." His smile was warm and his handshake firm and, after satisfying the details of what I was after, he looked at my feet and asked if I had a pair of "wellies."

"It's a wee bit damp down there," he said with a bit of the devil in his eye. "'Tis a ring surrounded by bog, so if you haven't got a pair, you'd best be taking mine."

I found myself at a loss for words as we moved to the porch where he pulled the knee-high rubber boots from his feet and handed them to me. He apologized for having only one pair, telling me he was due for tea in the kitchen anyway and would get along fine in slippers until I returned. Not knowing what to say, I gratefully accepted the still-muddy boots, placed them in the rear trunk of the car, and drove off in the direction he had indicated.

I located the site with little trouble and spent an hour or so in and around the stones. The guidebook was at least correct in its assessment of the site. The circle was in exceptionally fine condition, but as I photographed and noted the particulars it had to offer, my eyes were continually drawn to a lone spike of stone jutting hauntingly into the sky on the crest of a grassy hill some distance away.

After a time, I could not longer resist and I will admit that the experience was one not readily foreseen or forgotten. I walked up to the stone reverently, standing as it was all alone in the middle of a vast sea of green, and the stone, all fourteen feet of it, possessed all the magic and mystery I ever imagined. I walked around it clockwise, counterclockwise, stood, studied, and finally leaned into it hoping, almost expecting, to experience some great vision or sudden flash of energy. I closed my eyes and waited. The stone felt cold and coarse under my hands as I tried to envision the men who dragged its ten-ton mass the mile or more from its birth quarry before raising it precisely on this site. I imagined who, how, and wondered why they chose this particular place. I leaned against that stone all but begging it to speak, please, until all that was left was the wind blowing cold and wet down the back of my neck. The stone was indeed amazing, but the experience fell somewhat short of being magical and profound. There was no sudden electrical surge, no immediate sense of wisdom or power.

So I left. I grabbed my gear and took the first steps back toward the car and the farmer who thought well enough to lend me his boots. I turned around for one last look, facing the stone with far less hope and expectation, and that's when the true nature of the place revealed itself to me. With the wind and rain blowing harshly in my face, I realized at once how that stone, more dramatically than any surge or sudden flash, was everything basic and significant and human and godlike and was planted for everyone of all time to see. The magic was brought to light in the living, in the experience of being in that place, looking at that particular stone at that particular moment in time. My vision cleared and I felt myself open up. I saw that there was a balance to it all, to the hills and mountains, the grassy slopes and rock-strewn bog, and the elements that surged across it. I could see also that the men who erected this stone placed it exactly where it should be in relation to the lines and shapes of the landscape around it and around them. So pure, so simple, and still so much more than a stone. The integral part of that relationship aligns the earth with the heavens, the land with the men who live upon it, the past with the present. That stone, on that day, was about magic and mystery and the timeless relationship that binds a 5,000-year-old, 14-foot standing stone and a pair of lent wellies.

I'D BEEN PHOTOGRAPHING a particularly wonderful stone circle located in the center of a boggy field when it began to rain. It was a typical spring afternoon in the west of Ireland—heavily overcast with brief, though drenching, cloudbursts that blew in from the wild Atlantic. Normally, I just covered my cameras and hunkered under a waterproof parka until it quit. This cycle of on-again off-again was quite predictable and became a normal part of working and photographing on the Emerald Isle.

The farmer who owned the land provided me with some interesting details of the place, and I could see immediately that he hadn't exaggerated a bit. The grass outside the circle was close-cropped, while the grass inside was long and thick and appeared completely undisturbed. His cattle and long-haired sheep ate right up to the very outside edge of the ring, but, even though they could easily walk between the three-foot-tall stones, they simply would not go into the circle to feed. I'd heard of such places, but this was the first of only a few stone circles I'd encountered where the phenomenon was clearly evident.

After a time, the weather decided to turn against what I had come to consider typical and predictable about Ireland, and shortly the wind-blown rain began to fall in relentless sheets of ice-cold water. I gave up after twenty minutes or so and slogged my gear toward a sizable grove of trees at the far end of the field. Feeling defeated, but also as if some power were trying to drive me from the field toward something even more interesting, I slipped through the tree line and was stopped short in amazement by a large oak tree that loomed tall and ominous before me. More than six feet thick at the base, the tree had grown out of a rock wall that was part of a large ring fort and the monarch, big and as old as it was, had so much moss growing on it that the still-leafless upper branches did not allow the least bit of rain to reach the ground. I recognized it immediately as a tree of the *sídhe*, a place where fairies dwell, its magnificence rooted in and fortified by the ancient ring fort, a structure considered to be a vent to the Otherworld.

Ever-so-careful to disturb as little as possible, I set up the tripod and camera and shot a series of photos. The rain stopped shortly and, after giving thanks to the powers of the place, I completed my work at the stone circle and started back for the car and town. When I reached the farmers gate, he greeted me with a broad smile and an offer of a warm sitting room and a hot cup of tea. We talked long of our lives, exchanging tales and joking about those everyday particulars that keep life light and enjoyable. However, he became extremely tense and irritable as soon as I mentioned finding and photographing the tree.

"Ah, Jesus!" he began. "Tell me, please, tell me ye didn't mess with that tree!"

I got out only a word or two when my voice was cut off by his, "God man, I don't want my cattle go'n lame all because ye took photographs of that place."

He settled after a time, and I explained how, by my understanding of things, neither of us had anything to fear. In seeing the height of the grass in and outside the stone circle and, understanding the relationship between the tree and the ring fort, I recognized all these signs for what they were and left three silver coins under one of the roots before leaving as an appeasement for any trouble I may have caused the powers of the place.

"Thank God!" he said with relief. "Thank God there's one good Yank runnin' around Ireland who knows somethin' of the old ways."

Think what you like, consider it real or just superstition, but this man, a farmer in his mid-forties with a master's degree from Trinity College still respects and responds to the old beliefs despite his formal education. The rhythms and the expression of this ancient land speak the loudest at the end of a day in Ireland.

The wedge tomb stood well hidden in the maze of dense hazel and whitethorn that covers large sections of the otherwise stark magnificence that is the Burren. Finding the site was not

Brian McGrath and Wedge Tomb

as easy as expected even though my friend Brian had been there many times. The hazel was extremely tall and thick, creating islands between irregular avenues of sod, limestone, and the odd giant boulder. Brian commented on how overgrown these fields had become, and I asked why farmers didn't burn or at least cut the hazel to keep it in check. He said that some do, but added that the smart ones were extremely careful to never clear as much as they left. He explained that the hazel provides shade in the summer and a windbreak when the weather is foul, but I also recalled how other farmers told me that people in the Burren still respected hazel as a favored wood of the fairies and one was walking a fine-line when trying to decide how much of it the fairies were willing to lose.

We came around a large rock and I was stopped in my tracks by the sight of the tomb. Standing before me was the largest wedge tomb I had ever seen, and I was a bit surprised that none but a few locals knew it was there. I walked toward the opening and was stopped again when a patch of red fur fluffed by the wind caught my eye from the tomb's inner shadows. I waited for movement, but seeing none, stepped cautiously toward what appeared to be a big, beautiful fox lying across a large rock on the floor of the tomb. I touched him with a stick and was surprised to see that he was dead.

How strange it is when what's strange doesn't seem strange at all. Frost covered everything on that mid-March morning and the temperature had dipped well below freezing during the night. Yet the fox was not stiff, nor did he seem cold—it was as if he had been dead only a few moments. Even after looking into his eyes, so glazed and lifeless, the death was hard to accept considering his otherwise healthy appearance.

I worked my way into the chamber, inspected the body for wounds and, finding none, concluded that the fox had simply entered the tomb to find shelter during the night and had died. Never mind that we just happened by a few hours or moments later in that boulder-strewn maze overgrown with hazel and whitethorn that hadn't seen another human in weeks or months. When I looked around the interior of the tomb, the crescents and cup marks carved on the slab walls, things I've never seen on wedge tombs, seemed strangely natural as well.

NINE MILES OFF THE COAST at the southern tip of Kerry, two extremely large rocks rise out of the sea at such extreme angles you can hardly call them islands despite their size. The larger of the two offers only two places where a man can step from a boat to the cold stone, and then only when the sea is especially calm. The smaller offers no landfall at all and is inhabited by huge colonies of gannets, puffins, and other sea birds. Together they are known

The Skelligs

Skellig Michael

as The Skelligs, and sometime in the mid-sixth century, St. Finnán and a group of ascetic monks established a community on the largest island, naming it, Sceilig Mhichíl, in honor of Michael the Archangel. They built a small monastery with accompanying oratory and living cells in a saddle between the two main peaks more than 600 feet above the sea. They chipped and carved pathways in the rock faces from sea level up to the monastery in three places, one to a location that provides no landfall at all. There is also a stair of fourteen steps carved in the solid rock that leads nowhere—perhaps the product of someone's penance. They also built terraced plots where they were able to grow a few vegetables, mixing seaweed with what little soil they could find among the rocks. By some accounts, the monks also produced manuscripts similar to the *Book of Kells*, but no such artifacts have ever been found.

Vikings sacked the monastery several times in the ninth century, and many of the monks were lost to the sword. They were supported by members of the same order from a monastery located at Ballinskelligs Bay on the mainland, receiving supplies of bread and dried foods when the seas would allow for their transport in *currachs*, but basically they lived on birds, eggs, fish, and what little they could produce themselves. They had no heat, no source of fresh water other than what fell from the sky and, being as they were all there to suffer, must certainly have lived wonderfully miserable lives. They left the Skelligs for the mainland sometime in the twelfth century although for what reason no one is quite sure.

Ballenskellig Monastery

I've tried four times to get out to the Skelligs, once spending two days in Portmagee waiting in vain for the seas to calm. During the foot and mouth crisis of 2001, the Skelligs were one of the few monuments open to the public, and I'd been calling Des Lavelle, historian, naturalist, author, and skipper of a boat on Valencia Island, off and on for nearly two months hoping for word that the seas might allow a trip to the Skelligs. The weather during the last week of April had been mild and extended reports predicted the warmest, calmest days yet that year to happen the following Tuesday and Wednesday. Des said it looked good for Wednesday, so I got up at three a.m. and headed south to Kerry. Portmagee greeted me with bright sunshine, a free cup of tea from one of the pub owners, and an encouragingly calm sea. I had waited years to walk on Skellig Michael and this had to be the day. I felt it, Des assured it and, as we left the pier at half ten, all eight of us in the boat believed it.

But, it was not to be.

When we left the harbor, the swells coming in from the Atlantic were but a foot or two high. About half way to the small Skellig they grew to ten and fifteen feet with one occasionally larger than that. Des announced that the sea was too rough for a landing but recommended we carry on and at least get a look at the islands from the sea. Everyone except for a

Ballenskellig Cemetery

woman from Germany and myself was so seasick all they could do was moan. Des convinced everyone that the experience would be worth the pain. When we arrived at the small Skellig, we were met by roughly 27,000 pairs of snow-white gannets. The sky above was a massive swirl of wings, and every few seconds one of the birds would fold and dive headlong into the sea from a height of a hundred feet or more. Puffins and razorbills were bobbing all around the boat and the lower rocks were alive with seals. Although Des did his best to provide us with some extremely interesting information, he was blocked out by the sights, sounds, and smells of screaming seabirds and crashing waves.

When we reached Skellig Michael, most of us were fixed in a state of great amazement, although seasickness still dulled the shine on the faces of a few. Seabirds inhabit this island as well, but not nearly in the numbers as the small Skellig. Michael is, in fact, green, having grass, mosses, and wildflowers growing in the small patches of soil that lie here and there among the rocks. The pathways carved by the monks were all visible, and the beehive cells stood out distinctly in the saddle high above. There is also a lighthouse at one end of the island with a primitive helicopter pad beside it. We had to stay on the eastern side of the island because the waves coming from the west were growing ever larger, so we made one slow pass and then turned back toward the mainland.

Gallarus Oratory

Kilmacowen Standing Stone

The return trip was uneventful except for the huge rollers, the choppy waves in between, the wind, salt spray, and a fog that seemed to chase us the entire time. There were also the sounds of people moaning, groaning, and of course, heaving over the side. I survived intact, happily engaged in conversation with the German woman, a concert violinist from Mannheim. She asked what I as a writer had to say about what we had just experienced, noting that she sensed I had been somewhat overcome by emotion at the small Skellig. I sat silent for a while, trying to sort my thoughts. I told her then what I tell you now. I can describe every aspect of the scenes and acts I witnessed. I can speak of the history and what it must have meant to the men who chose to spend their lives on the edge of the world. However, as for the spirit, magic, and true power of the place, for me there are no words.

Fairy Tree with Castle Ruin

And living alone like this, alone with thoughts, concerns, dreams, and this thing called 'the project,' one begins to slip, not as if to go mad really, certainly not harmful or insane. But one begins to go wild, to sense things, not just see things, but to perceive more and more with every one of the senses the presence of things one would never have imagined encountering before. The intellect and so much of what is understood and appreciated logically is reshaped by what one comes to 'know' in this way. The madness is soothing, instructive and, in some, is but a step beyond brilliance.

Journal entry, Oughty, Co Clare, 4 May 2001

A Strange
Tale Indeed

EDDIE LENIHAN is as close to brilliance as anyone I've ever known. My association with him began in 1999 with a news story about the Fairy Bush of Latoon, a lone fifteen-foot whitethorn bush believed to be a gathering point for the fairies of Munster when they travel north to fight the fairies of Connacht. The fairies also stop at the bush on their return journey to assess their wounds and wait for stragglers. The bush stood directly in the path of a highway that was to be built between Limerick and Ennis, and Lenihan, knowing the stories surrounding the bush, wrote a letter to the local newspaper. He warned of revenge by the fairies if the bush were destroyed, and provided evidence from similar incidents to support his counsel. He was interviewed on a local radio station, and the story was picked up by Irish national radio and the New York Times. Media outlets all over the world carried the news, and Lenihan, backed by all this publicity, convinced the Clare County Council and the National Roads Authority to incorporate the bush into the landscaping of the new roadway, thus saving it.

Although this incident speaks strongly about Lenihan's character and respect for the Good People and their parallel world, it is only a hint of who the man really is. I believe that the one thing separating human beings from the rest of the natural community is the way in which we pass on information, especially things learned during a long and active life. This no doubt began with the very first hunters, the elder teaching the younger how to read tracks and predict the movements of prey. The mysterious images painted on cave walls many thousands of years ago look less like creative expressions and magical totems once you notice that the arrows and spears pierce only those points of an animal that would most effectively bring it down. The paintings undoubtedly served as instructional aids and were fashioned after stories told over and over by the oldest and most experienced hunters.

Fairy Tree of Latoon

Hence, storytelling is what separates us from the rest of nature, and Eddie Lenihan is a storyteller in the most profound and prevailing sense of the word. He has spent the last thirty years of his life collecting stories from elders in Ireland and is author of sixteen books, whose subjects include folklore, children's tales, poetry, and a history of the West Clare Railway. He has produced eleven audio tapes, a double CD, and travels to many different countries telling Irish tales. I had the good fortune to meet with Lenihan, and his wisdom and vast knowledge was one of the reasons I chose to live in County Clare in 2001.

He is intense, extremely involved, a guardian of the past who is always inspiring and entertaining. Yet, he is a man so humble he would not care to have me mention him at all. He represents a special kind of brilliance, weeding through the minds of the old people, recording another tale of the fairies or his much loved Fionn mac Cumhaill, looking for the Cursing Stones of Kilmoon, or simply asking how people fished the Fergus in the days before sporting stores. He walks about his beloved Clare with affection, respect, imagination, and just enough humor to appreciate the irreverence shown by whoever it was that placed the bright orange traffic cone on the head of the holy angel in the Ennis market square. He became a mentor of sorts to me, advising, instructing, and helping me work around the obstacles he knew I'd encounter along the way. He fed me with the care one gives a starving man, providing just enough nourishment so as not to ruin my appetite.

In the heart of the Burren stands an old ring fort. The high, dressed walls were built to suit the steep-sided hill they crown and, although the entire site seems lost in a sea of dense hazel, the structure stands out distinctly from several points along the road that passes below it. I had driven by the place countless times over the years and had always felt that someday a visit would be in order. Shortage of time or inclement weather had kept that from happening and a strangeness and melancholy I experienced every time I passed by caused me to be less enthusiastic than I might otherwise have been about stopping.

By the third or fourth day of my extended visit in 2001, I had already passed by the fort several times and had determined that late afternoon would be the best time to photograph the site. I believed I had all the time in the world, of course, but the foot and mouth restrictions shut everything down a few days later. Going into fields or forest, whether public domain or privately owned, was strictly against the law. There was no hiking or climbing allowed, and most national heritage sites were off limits as well. Fishing was allowed only from a boat at sea, and the government was prepared to shut down all the golf courses if the disease did in fact take root.

So there I was, a photographer living on a dairy farm with enough film for a year and all I could do was shoot from the roads. I was frustrated, felt cheated, but at the same time understood what was at stake and accepted my fate like so much bitter medicine. My presence was quickly known by nearly everyone in the county and although many of the farmers assured me I was no more infected than they, I honored the restrictions, kept a bottle of disinfectant in the car, and stuck to the roads.

What I came to jokingly call the 'fort of the strangeness' cried out to me each time I passed it. So, one crisp, clear evening as I drove down the valley toward the fort I came up with a plan. The farmer who owned the land directly opposite the fort was a man I knew well. He would not object to my trespass, I knew, so I decided to climb a hill on his side of the road and shoot across the valley into the fort. Everything went as planned and I headed back down the hill as the light in the valley faded with the end of day.

Suddenly, something streaked across the peripheral edge of my vision to the left. When I snapped my head around to catch it, something streaked across my vision to the right and when I wheeled in that direction there was yet another streak to the left. The manifestations had come from behind and shot past me down the hill toward the road. I could not put a name to what I had seen. They were streaks that appeared and disappeared in fractions of a second, but I could tell that they were light-brown in color and were perhaps four or slightly more feet in height. I stood dumbfounded for a time, not really frightened but certainly anxious over what I had seen. The next day I went to visit Eddie and described to him what had happened.

"Could it have been a badger, Tom?" he asked without so much as a blink.

"I don't think so, Eddie," I said. "A badger would only be knee high, and besides, these streaks were so fast . . ."

"Then how about a rabbit?" he interrupted, "There're some very big rabbits up in the Burren."

He wasn't mocking. He was leading me lightly through a questioning he clearly had been through with others many times. He ended by saying, "You try to find what in nature it could possibly have been and then if there's no explanation, you assume it was something that is just part of nature."

THE WEEKS FLEW BY and the foot and mouth restrictions remained in place. I carried my work to other parts of Ireland, but the feelings and mystery surrounding my 'fort of the strangeness' kept it ever in the back of my mind. Two days before I was due to fly back to the states, I could take it no more. The day was bright, sunny, and warm. I'd spent the entire morning photographing wildflowers in the Burren and drove down the valley toward the fort in the late afternoon. I was nervous, afraid of being caught, afraid of being injured, but more afraid of the regret I would feel if I didn't visit the fort. I drove by three times before I finally stopped and then as quickly as I could so as not to change my mind, I jumped the stone fence, ran through the thick hazel, scrambled up the steep slope, and found myself standing inside the fort near a collapsed section of wall.

Clearly built to fit the hilltop, the enclosure formed an irregular oval perhaps one-hundred-feet long by seventy-five-feet wide. The walls were nearly ten-feet thick and averaged ten to twelve feet in height. The interior grounds appeared to be relatively flat and were covered by moss and deep grasses. Not surprisingly, slightly off to one side of center stood a lone whitethorn bush around twelve- to fifteen-feet high.

I used a stick to poke and prod the grounds just in case the deep grass and moss concealed rough crags or fissures. Moving with caution and respect, I found the fort exhilarating and cheerless at the same time. There was a real sadness to the place; I could feel it in my bones, as if the shadow of some tragic event were seeping out of the rock walls around me.

Burren Stone Fence

On the other hand, the view of the Burren was incredible, and the late afternoon sun added warmth and dimension to the entire scene.

I had entered the fort by climbing the slope from the west. On the eastern side was a gateway about four-feet wide that led downward for a short distance to a narrow path of dressed stone that followed the curve of the hill both left and right into the dense hazel below. When I decided it was time to leave, I took the trail to the left and shortly found myself scrambling over broken rock in hazel and thorn so thick I had to shift and contort my body to make any headway at all. I moved down and around until I finally broke out of the rough. I found myself standing on a crumbled section of wall that opened once again to the grounds of the fort. I thought that a bit strange, never having had a sense of climbing upwards the entire time, so I went back to the gate and took the trail to the right. Down and down I went, pulling myself around tree and bush, and once again ended by standing in the deep grass of the fort.

I laughed, suddenly remembering a story I'd once read about another man whose curiosity led him into a similar situation. The powers of that place, the *sídhe*, were toying with me, but my intuition said that they intended no real harm. I walked calmly over to the whitethorn bush and pulled three silver coins from my pocket. I deposited them at the base of the bush and thanked the Good People for the day. Then I went back to the spot where I

Glenisheen Wedge Tomb

had originally entered the fort and started down the slope toward the car. I hadn't gone very far, however, when I was struck on the back by three hazel nuts that then rolled to a stop at my feet. I knew I was the only human on the hill that day, but the stinging sensation at three points of my back also let me know I wasn't exactly alone. Were the powers toying with me still? Were the three hazel nuts payback for the three coins I'd left or did they represent the sacred 'nuts of wisdom,' thrown at me in the hope that I might be made a little bit wiser? Whatever the reason, I took it all in good faith and appreciated the gesture. At worst, I'd resolved whatever fears I'd had over the fort, experienced firsthand the more playful side of the *sídhe*, and had a wonderful story to tell. I looked at the hazel nuts in the palm of my hand, deliberated a moment, and then buried them deep in the pocket where the coins had been.

A WEEK LATER found me stuck in stop-and-go traffic, four-lanes wide, bumper-to-bumper, with the temperature hovering somewhere around ninety degrees. South Denver seemed a long way from the Burren and, considering the pace I had lived over the previous months, these conditions came across as a very cruel joke indeed. Professional obligations had me driving thirty miles of inner-city freeways at peak times twice a day for over a month. Several of the people I had to work with were arrogant and intolerable and a number of long-term relationships I'd had with friends ended. The weather was hot and dry, yet I had a cold that would not go away. I was depressed, confused, often angry, but mostly sad. The 'project' fell by the wayside, and everything I'd written in Ireland lay ignored in a drawer of my dresser. My car often stalled in the heat and congestion of the freeway and once a perfectly good tire ran out of air. Every day brought another trial and every trial seemed to come a little more harshly. Sometime in July I literally felt my soul leave my body and it seemed all I could do after that was to try to hold on.

Fortunately, I awoke one morning from a crazy dream and immediately knew what was wrong. The hazel nuts should never have come back with me. They had been part of a manifestation of earth energies in Ireland, and that's where they should have stayed. I had deliberated and lost. In Ireland, at the base of that fort in the Burren, they'd had meaning. But here, they had become little more than props for a story. They were not even souvenirs. My actions had left them soulless.

I was not in a position to fly them back but I knew I couldn't hold on to them either. I phoned Eddie several times for advice but he was never home. A friend lent me a book that described a traditional 'round' designed to placate the fairies. The ceremony involved milk and a barren patch of ground, but another friend, one who professed to be an expert in Welsh Wicca, insisted that we bury the nuts in her garden following a baptism of wine. "Just trust me", she said, "I'll be responsible for any consequences." I stood by as she buried the nuts in a corner of the garden.

Almost immediately, my life got better. Work had me back in Boulder among people I knew and respected. My car stopped stalling, and friends came back around. I was about to punch the doorbell on the porch of a friend one evening when a large bird cast a shadow

Falls of Sídhe

that spun me around as it shot across my chest. My soul was back. My life became more creative and 'the project' was on again.

Shortly thereafter, I learned that the garden was dead. A year later, after fertilizing and replanting, everything, including the mint and rhubarb, plants almost impossible to kill, remained lifeless and brown.

I remembered the fort and all the experience brought me. I regret taking the nuts, but I'm grateful to have gotten my soul back. I also confess that much milk has been spilled in completing this project. The day before I left Ireland, I asked Eddie how the old people who claim to have seen the fairies describe their appearance. He pointed to the mule-eared likeness of a leprechaun on the cover of a book lying nearby and said, "Well, I can tell you they don't look a bit like that!"

He went on to say he's been told they stand four- to four-and-a-half-feet tall, are always young and beautiful, and have large, wonderful eyes. He added that anytime anyone gives him that description, he asks them if they recall what the fairies were wearing. "Always," he said, "they always respond by saying they can't recall or just never noticed." He went on to explain that for him this means the people are either lost to their beauty, or that fairies command little attention because they actually dress much the way we do.

I then asked him if he had ever seen a fairy. He looked at me for a time, ran his hand thoughtfully through his beard, and with the most Irish of sheepish grins said, "Well Tom, they're about four- to four-and-a-half feet tall. . . ."

Afterword

O3 MAY 1921—The Government of Ireland Act created the Free-State and partitioned Ireland. This left six of the nine counties of Ulster to be governed by the British from Stormont Castle near Belfast. The act was a key element in the agreement ending the Anglo-Irish war, and is considered the root cause of continuing problems in Northern Ireland.

In 1964, a militant Protestant minister and members of his congregation tried to enter Catholic West Belfast to remove the Tri-Colors, the flag of the Republic of Ireland, from the window of a vacant shop. Several nights of rioting between local residents and the police followed and, to many historians, The Troubles were officially born. Thirty-four years and 3,500 deaths later, many a journalist seeking relief from the cold the night of the Good Friday Agreement found promise in the sight of the Tri-Colors hanging on a wall opposite a portrait of Catholic hunger striker, Bobby Sands, in a room of Stormont Castle, itself the very symbol of British rule in Northern Ireland.

NINE THOUSAND YEARS of constant habitation have created an environment in Ireland like nowhere else on earth. From the raising of the very first standing stone, to the placement of an image of a contemporary Irish patriot on walls that represent oppression and persecution

'Mery Down

by a foreign country in occupation, the Irish race has been active in preserving all that is Irish today. Political divisions North and South are drawn by racial lines while the two Irelands, the earthly and the spiritual, defy explanation and the passage of time. Intuition provides a look into how the Otherworld is a very real part of the inherent makeup of the Irish character. The story is ongoing, never ending, and the current Troubles in the North are just part of the latest chapter.

The connection the Irish have with the Tuatha dé Danann, Tír na nÓg, and the Good People has worked hand-in-hand with respect for the land to preserve ancient monuments and archeological sites in remarkable numbers. Their story methods have provided a pre-history as pure and close to accurate as any culture can offer and the fact that British Prime Ministers are today apologizing for atrocities committed against the Irish over many centuries says something for the Irish people and their dedication to truth and justice. Yet, the Irish see themselves in history only as that history relates to their sense of place.

Identity for most Western Europeans and for descendents of Europeans who settled in other places is directly related to history, to time. There is a real point of beginning followed by repetition or points of abrupt change. In the six counties of Ulster Province, identity for Protestant Unionists and Loyalists begins in 1690 with the victory by King William of

Orange over the forces of Catholic King James II at the Battle of the Boyne. Their celebration of this event on the Glorious Twelfth of July is based on history, on time, and any sense of identity associated with the land comes from past and present links to Britain. They consider themselves members of the British race, and for them, Ireland is just another of the British Isles.

The same can be said for Irish Americans; identity began when they first reached America and developed over generations of living in a melting pot of diverse cultures. For the native Irish, however, identity is based on place, on space, and history is but one of the ways of confirming their experience with the land. They may appreciate that a standing stone was raised 5,000 years ago, but it is the existence of the stone and the people who raised it, and not the date it was raised, that is important to the Irish. They consider Ireland a completely separate island, independent and apart from all others. Likewise, they see themselves as a completely different race of people; they were spared Romanization, a feature that sets them poles apart from the majority of other tribes that make up Europe and the British Isles. The native Irish

In Drumoher Wood

Poulnabrone Sunset

are indigenous and therefore do not have the psychological burden of establishing their right to live on the land. What they possess is not so much an attitude as a quiet understanding that they are here today and have lived with the land forever. This takes them ever onward and the bones of their ancestors confirm all the right they need. Place generates time, but time is incidental and has very little to do with place.

Children dance for themselves, naturally and freely, until someone tells them to dance for others. It's then that they lose their innocence and become self-conscious. If one is happy doing what one does, one can go through his entire life without being aware that what he's doing is either different or special. Such is the case with the Irish.

Until recently, the Irish found little reason to question their status and position in the world. Being a society which is predominately rural, agriculture has been Ireland's primary industry for countless generations. Ireland has long had a reputation for producing the most disease-free livestock in the world. Other countries go out of their way to seek out the best breeding stock possible and, although less than ten percent of the population is presently involved in agriculture, Ireland has produced an economy that exports more than eighty percent of the livestock, meat, and dairy products it produces. The people in the country may mockingly refer to Dublin as London West and they may say that Dubliners have no idea what's going on in the 'real' Ireland, yet, as evidenced during the recent foot and mouth crisis and elections concerning which Eastern European counties should be included in the European Union (EU), the Irish know how to come together as one. They argue about the problems, come up with solutions, and simply get on with it.

Nevertheless, Ireland is changing fast. Membership in the EU is a double-edged sword that represents an economic blessing which may well be the undoing of much of what is considered uniquely Irish. Agriculture is quickly being dwarfed by industry. Brewing, textiles, clothing, and glass and crystal production have long been part of the economic scene and these, combined with the recent addition of chemical, pharmaceutical, machinery, transportation equipment, and especially software production, result in an eighty percent export rate that accounts for forty-five percent of the gross national product. Although these exports remain the primary engine for Ireland's rapid growth, the economy is also benefiting from a rise in consumer spending, construction, and business investment. It took a century and a half to reach prefamine population levels and everyone is working toward his share of the pie.

The extent of Ireland's growth was evident almost immediately after leaving the Shannon Airport in 2001. Following a two-year absence, the home construction business was booming, the traditional one-story Irish farmhouse was being replaced by two-story stone mansions whose design seemed more appropriate for the landscape of Germany, France, or suburban Oklahoma City. The narrow roads that demand expert driving skills in Ford Fiestas and Volkswagen Golfs seemed all the more narrow by a shift to oversized Mercedes and British-made SUVs. Noticeable also was the sudden introduction of No Trespassing signs in the countryside.

Most Irish farmers believe that everyone should have the freedom to enjoy the hills, meadows, and valleys that make up the landscape of Ireland. They see themselves more as caretakers of the land than the owners of exclusive rights and no one would ever tell another, neighbor or stranger, he couldn't cross the land to get to forest or sea. Such favor is as old as the land itself and is not in the least an exaggeration about the Irish. With the exception of the foot and mouth crisis, and I often had farmers apologizing for that inconvenience, I have always had free access to privately owned lands whether I was just walking or setting up to photograph a certain standing stone. The other side of that coin, of course, requires that I respect the place and it's keeper by closing gates and leaving the place unmolested.

But times and customs are changing. Since joining the EU, Ireland has had to create job opportunities and open up the country for sale to people from other member countries. Unfortunately, far too many of those moving in come with attitudes and biases that conflict with those of the locals. They do not adhere to the expression, "When in Rome . . . , " and, consequently No Trespassing signs are going up all over the place. Farms are being bought and broken up and the price of land has sky-rocketed. A three-acre parcel I looked at in 1998 for $11,000 sold for $260,000 in 2001 and the farmer was determined to sell even more. Many of the smaller farms help support themselves by accommodating tourists following an EU scheme that provides matching funds for the construction of self-catering vacation homes. While there is nothing inherently bad in this, some of the most greedy and unscrupulous farmers are building false dolmen and standing stones in an attempt to draw tourists to their farms and the great 'ancient' wonders they hold. This not only cheapens the true value of real monuments, it perpetrates an economy, especially among German, French, and other wealthy Europeans building summer and second homes faster than contractors can keep up, that is devastating Ireland's ancient monuments at an alarming and ever-escalating rate.

Silhouettes near Doolin

A process has begun that threatens to change the face of Ireland forever. Ireland had been a great center of knowledge from before the time of Christ until 800 years ago when the British invaded and started systematically eliminating anyone who would not honor the crown. Pliny the Elder had an Irish teacher, as did Virgil, Nero, Claudius II, and Gaius Julius Caesar. Devenish Island in Lower Lough Erne, Co Fermanagh, housed a university for druids and sages for hundreds of years and it was there, some historians claim, that Merlin took the babe, Arthur, to learn the skills of manhood and the wisdom of kings. The native voices who told Lady Gregory that all the great leaders of Ireland carry the blood of the Tuatha dé Danann in their veins spoke from a past that was rich and glorious. The new threat comes from forces a bit further than Britain, and it is my sincere hope, and that hope is colored by confidence, that the Irish will proceed into this new stage of history with a memory and leadership that provides the best of lifestyles while preserving all that makes the culture so unique and inspiring—the land, the stone monuments, and all who live in the parallel worlds.

False Dolmen

Doolin Pier

Benbane Head

River House, Dun McGrath

Cross of Carron

Dolmen at Knocknakilla

Acknowledgements

I
T WAS TWO YEARS AGO this morning that I drove the hundred or so miles to Ballenskellig Bay for a boat ride out to the Skelligs. Two years ago today that I got so close to the edge of the world I was almost lost to it. There was the wind and sea and a hundred thousand birds screaming at the gods.

Then there were tea and mussels shared in a pub with a couple who also knew they'd been changed but couldn't yet say just how. There was the grandmother telling stories at the bar, the baby on the bar stool, and later on, as I drove north in search of a cozy B&B, the wordless communication exchanged between myself and a fox trying desperately to cross the road.

I think another part of my soul returned this morning. I'm grateful but not sure I want it all back. Some of it must remain there. On the Skelligs. On the sea. In the hills and valleys and in the eyes of that fox.

Nothing happens by accident, and I must here thank all the people who have made this project and my life all the better. First and foremost, the McGrath family of Oughty, Kilfenora, Co Clare. They took me in, treated me like one of the family, and revealed so much of their lives to me. To Christy Brown for showing me the Burren, and to the farmer of Cathair Mhic Oirialla—we watched your cows and talked for hours but I never got your name. To John and Michael for their conversation and the occasional pint at Vaughan's, and to the people in and around Kilfenora for being so gracious and cooperative despite past experiences with curious authors. To Manuel, Laura, and the Donaghy kids for your ongoing support and love. To Trevor and Sheila Birney for their friendship and support; she, also, for the best dinner of our lives. To the Millers of the Ennis One Hour and John Kelly for your stories, advice and for allowing me to use your photo of Eddie Lenihan; you captured the soul of the man in a way I could only imagine.

opposite:
Cliffs of Moher

127

To Carolyn and Jan for your advice and editing skills; to David for your many talents; to Steve for being my champion while applying the pressure; and to each of you for being a good friend. To everyone at Amaranth for your support and professionalism these many years. A special thanks goes to Eddie Lenihan; of whom I cannot say enough; to Jan for your love and dedication; and to whoever touched my cheek on Emain Macha and changed my perspective forever.

A special thanks to Mickie Harkin for being the Irish brother I always wanted, and also to Dez of the Skelligs Service for his experience and love of the Rocks, and who, two years ago this morning, did his best to get me out to Skellig Michael even though most of the other passengers were heaving over the rail. To those passengers and to anyone whom I may have forgotten to mention, I do most humbly apologize.

Ogham Writing

Ogham Stone

Whitethorn and Stone Fence

Kylemore Lough

Springtime, Kilkee

Swans, Loch Inchiquin

Ballycullinan Lough Boat

Glossary

Aillén mac Midgna: The fairy musician who burned Tara every Samain for twenty three years

Angus Óg: Son of the Dagda and Boand

Ard Macha: Irish name for Armagh, two miles east from Emain Macha

ard rí: A title of honor for powerful leaders crowned at Tara

Badb: A supernatural woman who appears on the battlefield in the form of a hooded crow, one of the trio who make up the Mórrígan

Balor of the Evil Eye: A king of the Fomorians who never opened his eye except on the battlefield. Any army which looked at the eye became powerless.

Boand: Goddess of the Boyne River who had an affair with the Dagda to produce Angus Óg

Book of Armagh: A manuscript in Irish and Latin begun about A.D. 807 by Feardomnach in Armagh. Among other insertions, it deals with the lives of St. Patrick and Brian Boru.

Bres: One of the leading characters in the Second Battle of Mag Tuired, often referred to as Bres the Beautiful

Brigid: The daughter of the Dagda, associated with the feast of Imbolc, also one of Ireland's favorite Christian saints

Brug na Bóinne: Identified with Newgrange and may include Dowth and Knowth

Cesair: Queen of the first invasion of Ireland in the Mythological Cycle

Cnobga: Irish name for Knowth

Conchobar mac Nessa: King of Emain Macha and Ulster

Credne: A divine artificer of the Tuatha dé Danann

Cruachain: The great fortress of Connacht in Roscommon, the counterpart of Tara in Meath or Emain Macha in Ulster

Crunniuc mac Agnomain: The wealthy farmer of Ulster who wages that his wife Macha can outrun a horse

Cúchulainn: The greatest hero in early Irish literature and the principal hero of the Ulster Cycle

Dagda: The Good God, a leader of the Tuatha dé Danann

Danu: Mother goddess of the Celts

Dowth: A great passage-tomb in the Boyne Valley, with Newgrange and Knowth

druid: A priest of pre-Christian Celtic society

Druim Caín: A name for the Hill of Tara

Elcmar: The original master of Brug na Bóinne

Englic: One of the wives of Lug Lámfhota

Eochaid mac Eire: A king of the Fir Bolg

Fionn mac Cumhaill: Central hero of the Fenian Cycle and head of the Fianna Éireann

Fir Bolg: Early invaders of Ireland, coming after the Nemedians and before the Tuatha dé Danann

fulachta fiadh: An ancient cooking site

Good People: The fairies

Imbolc: Pre-Christian Irish feast day on 1 February

Knowth: A great passage tomb in the Boyne Valley, with Newgrange and Dowth

Land of Ever-Young: Tír na nÓg, the land given to the Tuatha dé Danann as settlement after their defeat by the Milesians

Lebor Gabála Érenn: Twelfth-century text also known as The Book of Conquests, or Book of Invasions

Lia Fáil: Irish name for the Stone of Destiny, the ancient coronation stone at Tara

Lóegaire Búadach: A hero of the Ulster Cycle along with Cúchulainn

Lug Lámfhota: Central hero of the Mythological Cycle of early Irish literature

Macha: (1) One of the trio of war-goddesses called the Mórrígan, with Nemain and Badb. (2) The wife of Crunniuc mac Agnomain after whom Emain Macha is named

Mag Tuired: Site of two battles between the Tuatha dé Danaan and their enemies

Medb: Warrior-Queen of Connacht and a leading figure in the Ulster Cycle

Milesians: The Celts, who defeated the Tuatha dé Danann

Mórrígan: The war-goddess made up of a trio of women, Badb, Nemain, and Macha

Mythological Cycle: A large body of verse, narrative, and romance centering on the successive invasions of early Ireland.

Nemain: One of the trio of war-goddesses who make up the Mórrígan

Nemedians: One group of early invaders of Ireland after Cesair and the Partholonians

Nuadu Airgetlám: King of the Tuatha dé Danann whose severed hand is replaced by one fashioned in silver by Credne.

Otherworld: The realm beyond human senses, the land of the *sídhe*

Partholonians: Early invaders of Ireland after Cesair from the eastern Mediterranean

ráth: An circular earthern fort, the residence of fairies

Samain: The November 1 pre-Christian seasonal feast

seanachie: A storyteller

sídh: A fairy mound

sídhe: The Good People of the fairy mound

Sliab Fúait: The highest point in the Fews mountains where Fionn mac Cumhaill and many others had numerous adventures

Sreng: The Fir Bolg warrior who cut off the hand of King Nuadu

Tailtiu: Name of the earth goddess who cleared the plains of Co Meath and asked that games be held there yearly after her death

Táin Bó Cuailnge: Oldest native epic in Western literature and the main text of the Ulster Cycle

Tara: Site of the Lia Fáil and seat of royalty

Teach Miodhchuarta: The Irish name for the banquet hall at Tara

Tír na nÓg: Land of Ever-Young

Tuatha dé Danann: The principal pre-Christian deities who invaded Ireland and went on to become the fairies.

Ulster Cycle: A large body of prose and verse centering on the traditional heroes of Ulster

Bibliography

Aalen, F.H.A., Devin Whelan, and Mathew Stout, eds. *Atlas of the Irish Rural Landscape*, 3rd ed. Cork: Cork University Press, 1997.

Brennan, J.H. *A Guide to Megalithic Ireland*. London: The Aquarian Press, 1994.

Brennan, Martin. *The Stones of Time*. Rochester: Inner Traditions International, 1994.

Burl, Aubrey. *A Guide to the Stone Circles of Britain, Ireland, and Brittany*. New Haven and London: Yale University Press, 1995.

Caldecott, Moyra. *Women in Celtic Myth*. Rochester: Destiny Books, 1988.

Cross, Tom Peete, and Clark Harris Slover, eds. *Ancient Irish Tales*, 4th ed. New York, Barnes and Noble Books, 1996.

Curren, Bob. *Complete Guide to Celtic Mythology*. Belfast: Appletree Press Ltd., 2000.

Dames, Michael. *Mythic Ireland*. New York: Thames and Hudson Ltd., 1992.

Delancy, Mary Murray. *Of Irish Ways*. Minneapolis: Dillon Press, 1973.

Flanagan, Deirdre, and Laurence Flanagan. *Irish Place Names*, 5th ed. Dublin: Gill & Macmillan Ltd., 1994.

Graham, Brian. *In Search of Ireland*. London: Routledge, 1997.

Gregory, Lady. *Lady Gregory's Complete Irish Mythology*. London: Chancellor Press, 2000.

Jacobs, Joseph, ed. *Celtic Fairy Tales*. London: Studio Editions Ltd., 1994.

Lavelle, Des. *The Skellig Story*. Dublin: The O'Brien Press, 1993.

Lenihan, Eddie. *Meeting the Other Crowd*, ed. Carolyn Eve Green. New York: Tarcher/Putnam, 2003.

MacKellop, James. *Dictionary of Celtic Mythology*. Oxford: Oxford University Press, 1998.

MacManus, Seumas. *The Story of the Irish Race*. New York, Wings Books, 1990.

Moody, T.W., and F.X. Martin, eds. *The Course of Irish History*, 10th ed. Cork: The Mercier Press, 1967.

Nelson, E. Charles, and Wendy Walsh. *The Burren: A Companion to the Wildflowers of an Irish Limestone Wilderness*. Dublin: Boethius Press and The Conservancy of The Burren, 1991.

O'Brien, Conor Cruise. *Ancestral Voices*. Chicago: The University of Chicago Press, 1994.

Rolleston, T.W. *Celtic Myths and Legends*. London: The Gresham Publishing Company, 1994.

Scott, Michael. *Irish Folk & Fairy Tales Omnibus*, 8th ed. London: Sphere Books, 1983.

Smyth, Daragh. *A Guide to Irish Mythology*, 2nd ed. Dublin: Irish Academic Press, 1988.

Westropp, T.J. *Archaeology of the Burren*. Ennis: Clasp Press, 1999.

Yeats, W.B., ed. *The Book of Fairy & Folk Tales of Ireland*. London: Chancellor Press, 2000.

Tom & Poulnabrone Dolmen

About the Author

Tom Quinn Kumpf grew up in a mixed, though predominantly Irish, working-class neighborhood in Pittsburgh, Pennsylvania. He served in the U.S. Navy in Vietnam and has since been deeply involved in conflict resolution and veterans' movements. He was part of a delegation of Vietnam veterans to visit Russia in 1990 and 1991, working with Soviet veterans of the war in Afganistan, and he has photographed many other areas of conflict in the world. He was drawn to Northern Ireland in order to explore the effect The Troubles have on the children there.

Tom has won numerous awards for his photography and his writing. *Children of Belfast*, published in 2000, was awarded a first place in design for the Western U.S. Book Design and Production Competition and was a finalist for the Pictorial Book Award of the Year for the Colorado Center for the Book. His images and essays have been published in many newspapers, periodicals, and magazines, including *Outside Magazine, Backpacker, Pravda,* and *Newsweek*. Exhibitions of his work are found in galleries and museums throughout the U.S. and Europe. *Irish Images*, published in 2003, is his inaugural series of postcard books. Tom lives in Boulder, Colorado.

The Wild Atlantic

The Irish Sea